Is individualized justice beyond the will or capacity of America at this time? In seeking an answer to this provocative question, Judge Polier suggests that it will be determined not only by how well law and psychiatry can learn to work together, but by how far America will enable the two to go in their response to its urgent social problems.

The courts have become increasingly concerned with individual rights, while legislation has become the main instrument with which this country seeks to solve its social problems. Paralleling this development, psychiatry has expanded its concern beyond the lone individual to the social problems that affect his mental health. Effective action in both fields, however, is blocked by dislike and fear of the criminal, the juvenile delinquent, the mentally ill, and the poor. These attitudes are reflected in inadequate support of legislative programs and lack of professional personnel to carry out such programs once enacted into law—proof of the vast gulf between society's pretensions and the reality of the protection it offers.

THE RULE OF LAW AND
THE ROLE OF PSYCHIATRY

The Isaac Ray Award Lectures

John Biggs, Jr., *The Guilty Mind: Psychiatry and the Law of Homicide*
Sheldon Glueck, *Law and Psychiatry: Cold War or* Entente Cordiale?
Justine Wise Polier, *The Rule of Law and the Role of Psychiatry*
Georg K. Stürup, *Treating the "Untreatable": Chronic Criminals at Herstedvester*

THE
RULE OF LAW
AND THE
ROLE OF PSYCHIATRY

by

Justine Wise Polier

Judge, New York State Family Court

*

The Johns Hopkins Press
Baltimore

For Shad, with love

PREFACE

I feel deeply honored to have been chosen by the American Psychiatric Association as a recipient of the Isaac Ray Award. No one working in either psychiatry or law can fail to appreciate the luminous contribution and the ongoing challenge of Dr. Ray to both fields.

In Isaac Ray one finds the rare and happy union of great intellectual power with boundless compassion. Like twin generators, each sparked, strengthened, and supported the other. His study of the causes of mental illness and methods of treatment moved him to apply what he learned to ease the miseries of the mentally ill. The suffering of the individual, in turn, drove him on in the restless pursuit of further knowledge. He sought to distinguish between those miseries that stemmed from the individual and those inflicted by society on the mentally ill. Old concepts, whether frozen into medical practice or written into law, did not escape his questioning.

Apart from Dr. Ray's major contribution to the question of when and under what circumstances insanity should be regarded as relieving a defendant of criminal responsibility, his writings raise questions with which the law and psychiatry are still wrestling. In a remarkable passage about capital punishment he wrote: "There can be no question which is most to be deplored, for shocking as it is for one bearing the image of his Maker to take the life of a fellow being with brutal ferocity, how shall we characterize the deliberate perpetration of the same deed, under the sanction of law and of the popular approbation?"[1] This question

[1] *A Treatise on the Medical Jurisprudence of Insanity* (1838), ed. Winfred Overholser, M.D. (Cambridge, Mass.: Harvard University Press, 1962), p. 147.

vii

raised in 1838 still remains unanswered in a majority of our states today.

In still another area Dr. Ray anticipated the functional school of legal analysis by nearly one hundred years. After noting that the insane were disqualified by law from appearing as witnesses in courts, he observed that a person might be regarded as insane for some purposes, such as the management of property if he should be senile, and yet might be treated as a trustworthy witness as to what happened at an earlier date. He gave other examples of accepted generalizations which were not in accordance with knowledge of the condition or the individual involved.[2]

Throughout his work Dr. Ray constantly reiterated his belief that his proposals could only be based on the knowledge available. He urged that the medical expert say he could not answer, that he would have to know more facts, that he needed more time for study and further consideration, rather than give an answer that might be wrongly interpreted or lead to injustice.[3] With controls so firmly rooted in professional integrity and personal modesty, he felt free to criticize the law for its failure to use the knowledge then available.[4]

Today, as in 1838, the limits of familiar concepts continue to fix boundaries of thought and action for men of both law and medicine. With the presentation by psychiatry of the role of unconscious forces as determinants of personality and action, judges, juries, and auxiliary staffs are often disturbed by concepts that raise questions as to accepted moral precepts. In view of the reception accorded Dr. Freud in Vienna by his medical colleagues, such reactions should not be surprising. The first exposure to a world of thought that seems to undermine the moral precepts as transmitted by parents, religious authorities, and the community produces many questions and conflicts, even among

[2] *Ibid.*, pp. 289–97.

[3] *Ibid.*, Appendix II. "Duties of Medical Witnesses," pp. 351–68.

[4] *Ibid.*, p. 13. In 1838 Ray wrote: "In their great zeal to uphold the wisdom of the past from the fancied desecrations of reformers and theorists, the ministers of the law seem to have forgotten that . . . the real dignity and respectability of that profession is better upheld by yielding to the improvements of the times and thankfully receiving the truth from whatever quarter it comes than by turning away with blind obstinacy from everything that conflicts with long-established maxims and decisions."

those endowed with intellectual curiosity and the will to learn. For the courts there is little opportunity for slow orientation. Can they comprehend such alien concepts? Will they be fearful and repelled, or will they attempt to explore and comprehend them? If they comprehend, will they be able to translate them into action?

There is also the danger of paying lip service to an appreciation of new concepts while acting as though they were non-existent. The outright rejection of psychiatry, the refusal to read psychiatric reports, the overruling of a medical finding of mental illness are today less common than they were twenty years ago. The process of rejection is now more subtle, but it remains pervasive in many areas through both action and inaction. In the words of Dr. Ray, "A new truth may be deprived of half its power by being mixed up with old formulas and venerable fallacies."[5]

To this warning one must add that the remaining half of the power of a new truth may also be lost where it is permitted to atrophy through non-application despite verbal acceptance. For this reason there is need to examine to what degree the non-application of mental health knowledge in our courts is caused by ambivalence toward psychiatry, with the result that its use is spotty, superficial, or a mere gloss. But we must also determine to what extent it is the result of the lack of essential personnel and resources or a reflection of entrenched opposition to social change. In similar fashion, it is important to determine to what extent psychiatry, fearful of the mystique of the law and distrustful of it as a constructive force, has chosen to remain apart from many of the grim and difficult human problems which confront the courts. Here we must examine to what extent the refusal to become involved is traceable to conditions in correctional institutions, state hospitals, and courts, which seem to defy the application of mental health principles and practice.

Except in criminal cases, in the days of Isaac Ray the law, as it affected insane persons, was primarily concerned with that

[5] From an article published in 1870 on the law of insanity, quoted by Dr. Winfred Overholser in his Introduction to *A Treatise on the Medical Jurisprudence of Insanity*.

small number of people whose competence either to manage or bequeath property was at issue.[6] Dr. Ray noted and challenged the differing standards of mental responsibility applied when conservation of property was concerned and when a man was charged with having committed a crime. He questioned why the law held a man responsible for a crime so long as he retained the slightest vestige of rationality, but deprived him of the management of himself and his property for far less serious or pervasive mental impairment.

> That a person whom the law prevents from managing his own property by reason of his mental impairment, should, in respect to criminal acts, be considered as possessing all the elements of responsibility and placed on the same footing with men of the soundest and strongest minds is a proposition so strange and startling, that few uninfluenced by professional biases, can yield to it unhesitating assent or look upon it in any other light than as belonging to that class of doctrines which, while they may be the perfection of reason to the initiated, appear to be the height of absurdity to everyone else.[7]

Despite the passage of almost 130 years since the publication of Dr. Ray's treatise, we have only begun to recognize that the quality of justice and of medicine should not be scaled according to the amount of property involved in a case or the financial condition of the person before the court or in need of psychiatric care.[8] Law and psychiatry are both rooted in the longings, aspirations, and fears prevalent in our world. Law is the work of many men who have sought answers to the question of how people can live together in society and handle their fears of one another.

---

[6] From the time of the Romans provisions for the protection of the property of the mentally ill preceded concern for the personal welfare of the mentally ill person. See The American Bar Foundation, *The Mentally Disabled and the Law* (Chicago: University of Chicago Press, 1961), p. 218, citing Albert Deutsch, *The Mentally Ill in America* (2d ed.; New York: Columbia University Press, 1949).

[7] Ray, *A Treatise*, pp. 23–24.

[8] See Jack Ewalt, M.D. (ed.), *Action for Mental Health*, Report of the Joint Commission on Mental Illness and Health (New York: Basic Books, 1961); Laurence C. Kolb, M.D. (ed.), "Report of the Special Advisory Committee on Psychiatric Services to the Commissioner of Hospitals, New York City," September, 1961 (mimeographed).

It has been used to control and to placate both those without power and those demanding more power. It has also been the instrument through which men seeking justice have sought to reshape social institutions. Psychiatry, as a branch of medicine, reflects the timeless efforts of man to heal the sick. At times, it, like law, has been an instrument through which society sought to restrain or conceal conditions in men that threatened or repelled it. It has also been the instrument through which men have sought to discover the causes of miseries that distort the mind and paralyze the emotions, so as to achieve individual and community health.

In the past half century law and psychiatry have both sought and had thrust upon them ever larger roles. The traditional concept that the primary role of law is to restrain individuals from wrongful conduct and to regulate or protect property interests is no longer valid, nor is the concept that the role of psychiatry is to determine criminal responsibility and provide restraint or care for the insane. Through legislation, judicial decisions, and administrative agencies, law has become one of the major instruments through which our society seeks to accomplish social change. In comparable fashion psychiatry, or the science of mental health, has become not only the source of special services for the mentally ill but a resource for solving and preventing many of the personal and interpersonal problems that plague our society.

At the present time, the expectations of the community are not matched by a commitment to provide the means or personnel for tasks of such dimensions. The roles of law and medicine will continue to be molded, if not transformed, by the necessities, the expectations, and the aspirations of our society. Both professions continue to be challenged with tasks which were undreamt of in former years. Each must, in its turn, challenge the community to enable it to fulfill its responsibilities. Psychiatry must correct old abuses, improve its skills, and extend its services so that no one will be deprived of them by reason of his economic condition. It must also increase its efforts to apply its knowledge of the individual to the broader problems that affect the lives of many individuals in society. It must become an effective force for the prevention as well as treatment of mental illness. Law must remove the abuses that have denied equal justice to the poor, and it must go even further. It must discover how it can become an instrument through which the enlarged concept of what is essential to the dignity, freedom, and fulfillment of the individual can be made a portion to which every man is entitled as a matter of right.

The role of law has been so greatly expanded in recent years that it touches aspects of life once regarded as completely outside its province. In different fashion, but also to an extent far beyond the expectations of medicine in earlier periods, the concepts of mental health and their application have influenced not only schools, hospitals, social agencies, the courts, and many other institutions which intimately affect the lives of people in this country, but our general thinking and approach to social problems. The rule of law and the role of psychiatry have grown and become interrelated simultaneously. To discover where each is going and how they can be mutually helpful in reaching the desired goals is a task which requires that they see each other as allies rather than as foes or strangers.

The chapters of this book were first presented as the Isaac Ray Award lectures at the University of Maryland in April, 1966. I am deeply indebted to the American Psychiatric Association, to the University of Maryland, to The Johns Hopkins Press for its encouragement and assistance, and, finally, to the Aquinas Fund, which has made the Isaac Ray Award lectures possible.

JUSTINE WISE POLIER

New York City
August, 1967

CONTENTS

THE RULE OF LAW AND
THE ROLE OF PSYCHIATRY

Chapter I

INTRODUCTION

Law and psychiatry still continue as two fields of knowledge and practice which seem far apart to the general public and to many practitioners of both professions. Fashions exist in law as in the social sciences. For a long period law resisted the intrusion of psychiatry into an area which its high priests regarded as sacred and not to be violated by experimentalists in human behavior. Psychiatry, except as it became directly applicable in determining questions of competence to administer property and of criminal responsibility, was excluded from the realm of professional concern. To the man of law, the psychiatrist appeared as an alien creature dabbling in something that was not a science and as a witness incapable of providing clear or definite answers to questions that required absolutes in an uncertain world.

In complementary fashion, the chasm between law and psychiatry was widened by psychiatrists, who, whether in a spirit of despair, frustration, or cynicism, concluded that the business of the courts was the administration of fixed rules and not a search for justice. To Dr. Gregory Zilboorg this is a possible explanation of why the courts were not concerned with securing or weighing scientific data.[1] This approach to law involves the image of justice as an abstract and fixed ideal, rather than as a goal that changes with modifications in the culture, the way of life, and the aspirations of a society. It fails to recognize how much easier it is to look back and to experience shock at ancient injustices

[1] Gregory Zilboorg, M.D., *The Psychology of the Criminal Act and Punishment* (New York: Harcourt, Brace, 1954), pp. 5–10.

1

than to challenge present ones and develop new concepts of how to order the affairs of men.

Dr. Zilboorg assaulted the long-prized "objectivity" of the law and saw it as a method by which judge and jury could comfortably remain at a psychological distance from the criminal. He criticized the law for its fear that psychiatry might understand the transgressor too well and might forgive too readily: "It is not really objectivity; it is more an effort to keep estranged from the criminal, to avoid knowing him, to look only on what he has done, on the act he has committed, to avoid any shortening of the psychological distance between the criminal and those concerned with judging and adjudging men."[2]

Unfortunately, the effort to keep estranged from the criminal is not limited to lawyers, judges, or juries. It reflects present community attitudes, which demand protection and accept the notion of punishment of the guilty as an essential deterrent to others prone to offend. It also reflects the uncertainty among psychiatrists and the community at large about the possibility of successful treatment of the "criminal," and the unwillingness of the community to invest heavily in such treatment.

These realities do not lessen the responsibility of psychiatry to seek to understand why the criminal acted as he did, to explore how criminal action by others can be prevented, or to discover what possibilities there are for helping the individual criminal to change so that he will not repeat his offenses. However, they do restrict the role of the courts, which must determine what the criminal has done and must enforce those safeguards the community requires for its protection at a given time.

Psychiatry cannot fulfill its responsibility to society by indulging in fantasies about what it may be able to do in the future. It has more to contribute to law than a diagnosis of a defendant's mental condition or a description of his past life. It may well be used to recommend the most helpful treatment and to predict the likelihood of recidivism. In considering what Kalven and Zeisel describe as "a future oriented role for psychiatry,"[3] it

---

[2] *Ibid.*, pp. 14, 39–41.
[3] H. Kalven, Jr., and Hans Zeisel, "Law, Science and Humanism," in Julian Huxley (ed.), *The Humanist Frame* (London: Allen and Unwin, 1961), pp. 331–44.

remains necessary for us to face the obstacles they acknowledge. These include (1) the psychiatrist's inability to convince
law of the effectiveness of therapy, and the unwillingness of the
psychiatrist to take responsibility for such therapy; (2) the high
cost of therapy, which society is as yet unprepared to meet; (3)
the threat to human rights involved in indefinite commitment
plus compulsory treatment; and (4) fear of taking on such fu-
ture-oriented responsibility on the part of law.

Too often, in discussing the limitations of the law in dealing
with problems of mental illness, psychiatrists emphasize only the
fourth obstacle. This oversimplification of the real difficulties is
an avoidance of responsibility for the other three, and leads to a
false romanticism about the role of the physician as against the
man of law.[4] It has also led to envisioning the conflict between
law and medicine as involving the issue of humanitarianism, in
which medicine has finally forced "the tempering of barbarity
toward the mentally ill."[5] This position has been based, at least
in part, on the attempts of a few courageous physicians to end
witch hunts against the mentally ill, to refute doctrines or dogmas
that proscribed the mentally ill as possessed of devils, and to dis-
credit physical torture as treatment that would exorcise the evil
spirits. Without detracting from the great contributions made by
physicians in these areas, it is important that we see them in perspective.

Barbarous punishment by men under the authority of law has
been challenged, through the centuries, by those who penetrated
the mask of legal justification for cruelty.[6] Dissenters who op-

[4] Dr. Zilboorg describes the physician as one trained to become empathetic
with people and their problems, and the lawyer as one trained to become emotionally estranged, both sociologically and professionally, from those who will
become his major concern (*Psychology of the Criminal Act,* p. 14). While
pleading for more understanding and differentiation among individual defendants, he makes his assertions apply to all lawyers and physicians. Both pic-
tures are false. In both professions, the whole spectrum of human strengths and
weaknesses is present. In both, one finds every variety of response to new concepts and every degree of resistance to change.

[5] Philip Q. Roche, M.D., *The Criminal Mind* (New York: Farrar, Straus
& Cudahy, 1957).

[6] Physicians who challenged accepted methods in the fifteenth and sixteenth centuries were challenging both church and state. In the sixteenth century Johann Weye boldly attacked law and lawyers for their role in the mis-
treatment of the insane. See John Biggs, Jr., *The Guilty Mind: Psychiatry and
the Law of Homicide* ("The Isaac Ray Award Lectures"; New York: Harcourt,
Brace, 1954), pp. 55–63.

posed cruelty under the guise of "legal punishment" have often had to suffer along with the objects of such punishment. Those who have accepted the decrees of their place and time either by implementing them or, by their silence, condoning them have always constituted the majority. This situation has held true from the earliest days of recorded history down through the Nazi period of three decades ago to the South Africa of today. Among the courageous individuals who have abhorred and opposed cruelty, one finds artists, physicians, and men of law willing to defy those in power regardless of the personal cost. Whenever the individual as a human being is moved by the unjust suffering of others, his special knowledge or gifts directed to the task, which seems overwhelming, may be used in a way that lends great meaning to his efforts.

Progress in developing a more sympathetic understanding or relationship between law and psychiatry has also been held back by an assumption widely held by physicians that law can only affect the external conditions of the mentally ill, while psychiatry alone can effect the internal changes essential to healing. This position, while flattering to medicine, has at times led to condescending attitudes which have alienated men of law charged with controlling overt antisocial behavior. It fails to recognize that, just as scientific knowledge can introduce new understanding into the field of law, society through law can modify not only behavior but attitudes and interpersonal relationships.

For a long time we were told that the prejudice and discrimination practiced by majority groups in this country could only be changed in the "hearts of men." However, in the past twenty years we have learned that when law is used to end discriminatory practices resulting from prejudice, prejudice may also be modified. To see the agencies of justice as only "agencies of counter-aggression against the aggressor called a criminal"[7] projects a false image of the role of law in a democratic society. As society changes and those who have the power to make and enforce laws reflect or project increasing concern for the well-being of larger and larger numbers of individuals, there is in

---

[7] Zilboorg, *Psychology of the Criminal Act*, p. 75.

law, as in medicine, a reaction to this expanding concern for members of our society as individual human beings. The result has been not only more humane punishments but a growing preoccupation, among members of both professions, with the causes of deviant behavior and the possibilities of treatment and preventive measures. The zig-zag of action and inaction reflects the limitations and anxieties of those charged by the community with control. It also reflects both satisfaction and dissatisfaction with punishment for its own sake.

Progress made by both professions has been interrupted because new insights concerning the individual defendant or mentally ill person have illustrated the problems of not one individual in court, clinic, prison, or hospital but of thousands, seen and unseen. In turn, because of the scope of the problem, society has been unprepared to apply either through law or medicine what we have begun to understand. Apprehension over the size and cost of changing our vast institutions conflicts with the growing awareness of the need for individual consideration of patient or defendant. While we reach for humanization of community life so that each individual will be accorded a sense of dignity and worth, we are drawn by the sheer weight of the new problems into building institutions and providing makeshifts that negate this goal.

In turn, the inability of society to cope with the size of the problem has played into the hands of those of its members fearful of change and hostile to the use of scientific knowledge. Such persons resist all questioning of the effectiveness of the traditional use of punishment. The formalized and sanctioned power to judge and punish, like the divine right of kings, is not only jealously protected by the comparatively few with power but also by those without it—those who either identify with it or rely on it to keep the sun in the heavens.

In addition to these factors and attitudes, there are also more personal attitudes on the part of both psychiatrists and lawyers that have created hostility, misunderstanding, and lack of mutual respect. The psychiatrist generally regards the lawyer as a necessary evil in his own life, who takes care of leases and wills. He is the undertaker of dying and dead marriages, who may, with heavy hand and aggressive harassment, seek to force an advantageous settlement of property rights for his client. He is the advocate who demands yes-or-no answers to impossible hypothetical questions at the investigation of a man's sanity, or engages in a bitter battle for the custody of children without regard for their welfare. The lawyer, in turn, is likely to place psychiatrists in one of two categories: those eminent and reluctant dragons who will do anything to avoid court appearance but who, if ensnared, add a new dimension to the problem at hand, and those eager and ready to come to court as experts, whose testimony can be contradicted at all times by others equally eager to testify.[8]

To what extent these negative images of lawyers and psychiatrists reflect old prejudices, false assumptions, or kernels of truth is certainly of less significance than are the stirrings in many areas that should do much to create new understanding and cooperation. There are many forces in our society that are serving as catalysts for change. Young lawyers are being introduced to the world of psychiatry through studies at college, through books, through plays, and, all too frequently, through personal family tragedies involving mental illness. In medical schools, in internships, in residencies, and in graduate training, young psychiatrists are being exposed to the family and social problems that have shadowed the lives of their patients.

One hopes that this does not mean that a new breed of professional man is being developed who, like a zebra, will have streaks of law and psychiatry interlaced throughout his speech or embroidered on his outer garments. It does, however, mean that law, which expresses society's decisions as to the ordering of human conduct and relationships, and psychiatry, which seeks to prevent or heal mental illness, are becoming more closely interrelated through the growing knowledge and experience of members of both professions.

There are still other reasons why the professions of law and psychiatry should have each remained so egocentric in dealing

---

[8] Manfred Guttmacher, M.D., *The Mind of the Murderer* (New York: Farrar, Straus & Cudahy, 1960), pp. 118–19. Dr. Guttmacher approves the statement of Chief Judge Emory Niles of the Supreme Bench of Baltimore that our system of using partisan expert witnesses has alienated the best, while we accept and are shocked by the performance of the worst.

with the other. Law regarded its niche as well established by tradition, precedent, and the specialized knowledge required for its application. Psychiatry, a stepchild of the medical profession and an object of suspicion to the lay world, moved in a special ethos and by the process of exclusion and self-exclusion created its own ghetto walls. In addition, the special and limited areas in which there was confrontation or mutual involvement of law and psychiatry gave added reason for what might be called arm's-length transactions or mutual suspicion. To psychiatrists law was an institution that applied fixed and rigid rules concerning moral responsibility for criminal action and was incapable of seeing the criminal as an individual. The courts were seen as prating of their concern for the best interest of the child while chained to moralistic and religious conventions that permitted little consideration for his healthy mental and emotional needs.[9] Lawyers were seen as manipulators of the psychiatrist, concerned with securing certain answers to questions that demanded sensitive, ongoing scientific exploration. When psychiatry expanded to explore the developmental history of the individual and his unconscious drives and motivations, the sorry caricature of preoccupation with sex increasingly threatened the bastions of law, which had long provided a refuge for ivory-tower illusions of certainty as to the responsibility of man for his actions. After World War I, the resistance to psychoanalysis was transformed into an all but self-flagellating embrace in certain circles. Social workers sought to become junior analysts; educators saw themselves as child therapists; and some members of the legal profession began to parade a clinical jargon which formerly would have made them suspect among their peers.

[9] See Anna Freud, "Psychoanalytic Knowledge of the Child and Its Application to Children's Services," Address to Citizen's Committee for Children of New York, April 6, 1964 (mimeographed), pp. 14–15:
Family Law so far as it deals with the provision made for minors in divorce, adoption, custody proceedings, has been oriented always with regard to the best interests of the child, which to the Court seemed safeguarded if the child's religion, morality and financial security were protected. . . . The "best interests" of the child are served best, according to analytic experience, if his emotional needs rather than his religious and moral concerns are taken into account.

Now we are engaging in what we believe is a more realistic approach to joint ventures that require concern and service from law, social welfare, and psychiatry. Law is increasingly concerned with the mental and emotional problems of individuals. Psychiatry is increasingly concerned with the external world of reality for patients and the society which produces the sick, the emotionally disturbed, or the non-productive individual. A new mutual regard and healthy cooperation are beginning to emerge in place of the resistance, hostility, mutual suspicion, condescension, or false reverence that prevailed in earlier periods. In this more friendly atmosphere there is greater reason for the re-examination of the roles of law and psychiatry than at a time when law angrily rejected psychiatry and the infatuated devotees of psychiatry saw it as the answer to all human problems.

The extent to which this new cooperation will become an effective force in the lives of people will not depend only on the changing winds of fashion, but largely on the readiness of the mental health professions, through insights, experimentation, research, and service, to become truly available for tackling the momentous social and human problems with which the law must grapple. Although the intellectual climate now invites the contribution of mental health to law, repeated unavailability and resulting frustration can have disastrous effects on that climate and on progress in coping with men's problems. Experiments that cannot be evaluated through research, replicated, or broadened in scope because of lack of trained personnel or funds provide a source of constant discouragement, as law turns to science for more than a diagnostic opinion and seeks help in designing laws and procedures for the treatment and rehabilitation of troubled human beings.

There are hopeful signs that such barriers can be lowered. The newly felt need to correct the social conditions which have denied opportunities for healthy development to children of the poor and of minority groups has touched the lives of many young people in different disciplines. Social workers no longer feel that in order to become "professional" they must act or be regarded as quasi-psychiatrists. Teachers no longer feel that to achieve status they must become experts in child guidance. Psychiatrists are beginning to recognize the challenge of work in the state hospital or community clinic and are ceasing to feel that their highest ambition can only be fulfilled by being glued to a chair, supported by a couch. Lawyers are becoming aware that reputable or successful practice need not be confined to business problems, and that the role of law in discovering and enforcing the rights of men is worthy of their best efforts. Our troubled world has created more than one type of young rebel. More young people have come to view professional services as no longer of lower status than those occupations directed to the manufacture of things or what goes under the general rubric of business.

It has been suggested that whenever a society is relatively relaxed, the opportunities for social experimentation are greater, whereas in time of acute stress we pay less attention to the individual and tend toward "crash programs."[10] It would seem rather that in times of stress the work directed to healthy development of the individual is limited to a small and deeply committed group. When the larger community becomes concerned, it discovers how much is known that has not yet been applied, and can reap the harvest of years of unnoticed work.

The law cannot call on psychiatry for unscientific absolutes, for certainty rarely exists in human affairs. But it can be called on for knowledge, searching insights, and creative planning in the affairs of our society. The need of law and society is not for control by but for maximum contribution from this science, as well as from other natural and social sciences.

The evolution of psychiatry as a science concerned with the mental health of the individual and the society of which he is a part must go hand in hand with the evolution of law as an institution which regulates the conduct of the individual and develops social institutions through which the welfare of society can be strengthened. Evolution in both areas will depend on the development of knowledge through experimentation, research, and application of what is learned. Psychiatry can no longer justify its absence from, or occasional appearance for a specific purpose

---

[10] See Rudolf Ekstein and R. L. Motto, "Psychoanalysis and Education, an Historical Account," *The Reiss-Davis Clinic Bulletin*, I, No. 1 (Spring, 1964), 7–23.

in, the field of law on the ground that it is individual-centered, whereas the law is public-centered. It can no longer regard itself as a discipline susceptible to constant change in the light of new knowledge, and yet see the law as a fixed and rigid institution unrelated either to changing social problems or to the individual's needs within a changing society. In turn, law can no longer justify its failure to reach out and apply knowledge from psychiatry on the grounds that legal terms are precise and that the definitions and terms of psychiatry are too vague or too nebulous for application in legislative halls or courts. The legal definitions of the mentally ill exceed the psychiatric definitions in number, variation, and vagueness.[11]

Those engaged in the field of mental health have expressed increasing concern during the past decade about the "alienated" man, the man without a sense of his own identity, the man without sufficient sense of purpose to be motivated to function effectively or happily. Whether in response to this concern or to other stimuli, law has, in its own way, addressed itself to the same problem, or at least to some of its symptoms. Legislation has been enacted to provide more benefits to more individuals in our society as a matter of right. It has also addressed itself to problems of individuals who express their alienation from participation in the work and life of the community in different ways. These include criminal behavior, alcoholism, narcotics addiction, and mental illness.

As we look back on the rule of law as interpreted and reinterpreted by our courts during the past few decades, we see that it has passed through the state of self-alienation to increasing involvement in the problems of society. It has accepted respon-

---

[11] See The American Bar Foundation, *The Mentally Disabled and the Law*: "Current advances in psychiatric knowledge, such as the more accurate use of medical terms, have not appreciably eased the difficulty of relating that knowledge to the law. Perhaps an explanation may be found in the diverse purposes of legal and medical terms. *A legal term has a precise meaning which may not coincide with popular, religious or scientific concepts*" (p. 3; italics mine). Only slightly later in the same Preface, the authors write, "*One of the major sources of confusion in the law has been the use of vague and nebulous descriptive terms*" (*ibid.*, pp. 3–4; italics mine). Later in the volume it is noted that in twenty-seven states there are twenty-eight distinct and separate legal definitions of a psychopath.

sibility for interpreting the constitutional provisions for equal protection under law and the right of due process to encompass groups formerly disenfranchised and burdened by many forms of discrimination. Courts are beginning to pierce not only corporate veils but governmental and institutional structures that appear to grant equal justice or opportunity to groups or classes but that, in fact, fail to do so. Perhaps most significant is the increasing emphasis placed on what makes "rights" meaningful, so that the shadow or color of rights shall not be substituted for the reality. Recent decisions interpreting the "right to counsel" as more than a nominal right for the poor[12] and giving meaning to the prohibition against forced confessions[13] are but two examples.

In this development of judge-made law, procedural forms take second place, and the question of whether justice was done in regard to the individual takes priority. In order to determine whether the individual has received fair treatment, the courts have become far more ready to examine the factual dispute underlying the constitutional questions involved.[14] It is significant that this trend, despite all complaints of federal interference and fear of the additional burdens that will be placed on the courts, reflects a growing awareness that the quality of justice cannot be seen as separable from its effect on the individual involved. In the words of Judge Schaefer, "Even with the narrowest focus it is not a needle we are looking for in these stacks of paper, but the rights of a human being."[15]

[12] *Gideon* v. *Wainwright*, 372 U.S. 335 (1963). The extension of the right to counsel in criminal cases was extended to mental patients as a constitutional right by the New York Court of Appeals in *People* ex rel. *Rogers* v. *Stanley*, 17 N.Y.2d 256 (1966). See also *Rollerson* v. *United States*, 119 U.S. App. D.C. 400, 407; 343 F.2d 269, 276 (1964): "When the community fails to supply—for those who cannot—the effort and resources required for an adequate exploration of the issue, the trial becomes a facade of regularity for partial justice."

[13] *Escobedo* v. *Illinois*, 378 U.S. 478 (1964).

[14] See Abraham D. Sofaer, "Federal Habeas Corpus for State Prisoners: The Isolation Principle," *New York University Law Review*, XXXIX, No. 1 (January, 1964), 78–135.

[15] Walter V. Schaefer, "Federalism and State Criminal Procedures," *Harvard Law Review*, LXX, No. 1 (1956), 25.

While law, through social legislation, is enlarging the scope of governmental action that will affect ever more people, judge-made law is showing increasing concern for the rights of the individual. These complementary approaches to the rule of law as it touches the lives of individuals have brought law closer to psychiatry and to all social sciences concerned with the health and welfare of people. This closer relationship, in turn, has led to greater understanding and mutual reinforcement. At times it has also led to misunderstanding and even sharp conflict, based on differences in perceptions as to goals, practices, and inter-pretations of both individual and societal rights.

The changing nature of our society and the demands made on both law and psychiatry require a re-examination of the role of both, and also of their relationship to one another. The changes require that those institutions financed by government to meet the needs of people (such as law, education, health, and welfare) shall become more concerned with the welfare of the individual.[16] At the same time, medicine and psychiatry, long regarded as sciences directed toward the welfare of the individual, must con-cern themselves with the welfare of society in far broader terms.

With these two necessary developments, which are not yet clearly defined or articulated and which now move forward by starts, jolts, and stops, we find differences of pace, contradictory and conflicting positions, and great gaps in performance. These differences and conflicts are not limited to the relationship be-tween law and psychiatry. They are part of the more basic con-tradictions that must be resolved as traditional institutions and procedures are re-examined and modified to meet the needs of a democratic society, as we see those needs today.

This is no easy task. It is paradoxical that while the notion of the affluent and great society makes possible expanded legisla-tion for the welfare of the individual, the complex bureauc-racies and the conflicting interests of those who hold the power

---

[16] See Charles A. Reich, "The New Property," *Yale Law Journal*, LXXIII, No. 5 (April, 1964), 733–87. Professor Reich points out the growing control over property by government through its emergence as a major source of wealth and its growing influence in the lives of individuals. See also Elizabeth Wickenden, "Social Welfare Law: The Concept of Risk and Entitlement," *University of Detroit Law Journal*, XLIII, No. 4 (April, 1966), 516–39.

of wealth or the power to administer wealth have constituted sources of restrictions upon the individuals whom the laws are intended to benefit. Such restrictions on individual freedom come from many sources. First is the inability of the individual and the unwillingness of society to challenge those institutions (whether governmental or subsidized by government) which have been vested with the power and duty to aid people. A second and no less serious source of restrictions lies in the general acceptance of the vast gap between the pretensions of society as to its commitments and what we are in fact prepared to do or spend to achieve our goals.

The old concept that legal disputes arise when differences are perceived between parties also holds good on the newer and larger stage, where differences are perceived between the welfare of the individual and of the community. Both law and psychiatry have an important role in encouraging and developing the perception of such differences and in helping to resolve the resulting disputes.

There is a good deal of circular reasoning in the writing of physicians, lawyers, judges and others as they struggle with the question of who shall and who shall not be held criminally responsible for his acts. As more is learned about the mind and the emotions of man—as their relationship to what he does and the forces that influence or control his development are identified and clarified—old assumptions, opinions, and precedents are subjected to new scrutiny. Uncertainty abounds, to the discomfort of all, while new knowledge and new concepts struggle for acceptance.[17]

Society's tacit agreement that a mentally diseased person should not be held responsible for his acts and that a person

[17] I shall not deal with the questions of lack of testamentary capacity, ability to make a valid will, or procedures for commitment to a mental hospital and commitments of defective delinquents or of those who are so mentally defective as to require state care. These areas, in which law and psychiatry both have a role, have been studied in the Isaac Ray Award book by Winfred Overholser, M.D., *The Psychiatrist and the Law* (New York: Harcourt, Brace, 1953).

held responsible should not be regarded as mentally diseased provides a form of circular reasoning that fails to supply answers to the questions that confront law and psychiatry. The issue is of how greatly impaired a person's sense of reality, his response to the outside world, and his ability to control his conduct must be for society to declare that he is not criminally responsible and is in need of medical care rather than punishment.

Medical opinions have differed in regard to organic psychoses, schizophrenia, manic-depressive psychoses, and various psychopathies. The result of these varying psychiatric diagnoses and opinions has been disagreement as to what degree of mental illness relieves an individual of responsibility for his actions.[18] Both the courts and the larger society sense that these opinions reflect not only medical but social judgments as to whether the areas of non-responsibility should be enlarged and whether it is prudent to broaden the gray or uncertain areas that may obscure "definitive" guidelines applicable to specific cases. Some physicians have expressed apprehension that an ever-widening "gray" area is being created in which "criminals" will be able to inflict injury without being called to account.[19] This uncertainty among the experts as to where lines should be drawn reinforces resistance to change in a culture that demands clear differentiation of right and wrong.

The expectation of or demand for exact yardsticks from psychiatrists upon which results can be measured is in sharp contrast with the lack of similar standards for the legal profession. The extreme variations in "justice" that exist are often dependent upon which judge sits and which lawyer tries a case.

[18] See Robert Waelder, M.D., "Psychiatry and the Problem of Criminal Responsibility," *University of Pennsylvania Law Review*, CI, No. 3 (December, 1952), 378–84.

[19] Dr. Thomas Szasz has become the leader among those taking this position. In *Law, Liberty and Psychiatry* (New York: Macmillan, 1965) he pleads for liberation from psychiatry and alleges that the "rule of law is threatened by many contemporary psychiatric practices." Indeed, he declares, "the notion of mental illness has outlived whatever usefulness it may have had and it now functions as a convenient myth. . . . I am not saying that personal unhappiness and socially deviant behavior do not exist; but I am saying that we categorize them as diseases at our own peril" (pp. 6–7, 16–17, 137); see also Ronald Leifer, "The Psychiatrist and Tests of Criminal Responsibility," *American Psychologist*, XIX, No. 11 (November, 1964), 825–30.

To say that compensation must be "just," the protection of the laws "equal," punishments neither "cruel" nor "unusual," bails or fines not "excessive," searches and seizures not "unreasonable" and deprivation of life, liberty, or property not "without due process" is but to give a formulation to the lawmaking activity of judges, left free to define what is cruel, reasonable, excessive, due, or for that matter, equal.[20]

Expert court testimony which seeks to illuminate and explain the causative chain that led to certain behavior or criminal action has been caricatured as representing the doctrine of *tout comprendre, c'est tout pardonner* rather than as evidence to be weighed in determining sanity, responsibility, need for hospitalization, or the appropriate sentence. Therapy is too often portrayed as a form of permissiveness that reflects softness, instead of as the disciplined use of scientific knowledge. The fact that throughout the centuries harsh punishment has been proved to be a failure as a deterrent has failed to prevent the imposition of such punishment when ugly crimes inflame public passions. Such punishments all too often only provide vicarious satisfaction to the public or meet some unconscious need for their imposition on the part of judge or jury.

Instead of being seen as the expert who can present knowledge to be accepted or rejected by the courts, the psychiatrist is expected to assume two conflicting roles. He is too often blamed if he fails to be both the scientist presenting the knowledge of his field and the citizen who is expected to pass judgment on the defendant. By making the issue seem more complex than it had originally, by raising doubts in the minds of judge and jury as to what should be done, by lessening their confidence in their own judgment, the knowledge that the psychiatrist places before the court may arouse resentment. Judges and members of the jury, being human, can turn away from and resent things they do not understand, especially if new elements of uncertainty are added to what is at best a difficult task—the judgment of another human being. Psychiatric explanations of repulsive crimes are brushed aside, and are often interpreted as excuses. Prevention of

[20] Alexander H. Pekelis, *Law and Social Action, a Jurisprudence of Social Welfare* (Ithaca, N.Y.: Cornell University Press, 1950), p. 4.

punishment in such cases violates the "personal ethic" and the confidence in the moral culture in which we have been nurtured, where "good" and "evil" remain opposites.

If physicians are to remain physicians, should they be asked to do more than give the patient's history, the diagnosis, their opinion as to how the medical condition may affect his action, and the prognosis for future behavior? If courts are to fulfill their role, have they the right to ask physicians to determine or give opinions on the question of legal responsibility, which, as the cases show, changes from state to state, from county to county, and, within the same geographical areas, from decade to decade? Dr. Willard M. Gaylin writes that whenever "a psychiatrist testifies in an insanity defense he is doing so not under the *M'Naghten* or *Durham* rules, but under the rule of the impossible. . . . guilt and innocence, as used in the criminal law, are not functional concepts in psychiatry."[21] He sees the role of the psychiatrist as properly limited to advising on what should be done to or for the man who has violated the law and on what punishment would be most effective and would discourage recidivism. These are the areas of perception, behavior, and learning to which his knowledge, training, and experience are relevant.[22] Such a withdrawal from the tough process of decision-making may remove the "scientific crutch" from judge and jury as they face the task of acting under "the rule of the impossible." However, one must

[21] Willard M. Gaylin, M.D., "Psychiatry and the Law," *Columbia University Forum*, VIII, No. 1 (Spring, 1965), 23–27.

[22] See John Biggs, Jr., *The Guilty Mind*. Judge Biggs refers to a report of the Group for the Advancement of Psychiatry, which sees the role of the psychiatrist as one of predicting with some accuracy the "deterrability" of the accused individual, and notes: "This is an important fact, for if psychiatry can inform the law as to those offenders who may be deterred from further crime by limited imprisonment as well as those who should be permanently institutionalized, a field becomes apparent in which cooperation between the law and psychiatry can yield most desirable results" (p. 170).

Dr. Sheldon Glueck reports that in Massachusetts the use of the services of an impartial psychiatrist appointed by the Department of Mental Hygiene to evaluate the defendant has made it possible to discover the mental aberrant before trial in some cases. He states that as a result of the procedure if the examining psychiatrist finds the defendant to be "sane," the defense of insanity is rarely raised at the trial. A third beneficial result is seen in the reduction of conflicting expert testimony (see *Law and Psychiatry: Cold War or Entente Cordiale?* [Baltimore: Johns Hopkins, 1962], p. 139).

also question how the psychiatrist's absence from the battle or above-it-all-stance will correct or improve traditional concepts of responsibility within the administration of law.

While Dr. Manfred Guttmacher recognizes that at times the expert witness himself is responsible for the unhappy situation in which he finds himself, he vividly describes the reasons why the physician finds the whole trial process both alien and bewildering. The process does not permit insistence on the patient's whole history, the questioning of witnesses, or consultation in search of truth. The expert ceases to be his own master and is subject to questioning that seeks to impugn both his competence and his integrity. Finally, he is expected to act as a partisan.[23] Judge Bazelon has pointed out that the presentation of relevant information is the duty of experts. It is, however, the task of the community represented by the judge and jury to act, to render the decision. He believes that doctors find it hard to accept this limited role. While one may ask what courts know of mental illness, one may also ask what doctors know of due process, the right to counsel, *habeas corpus*, and the like.[24]

In fairness, it must be acknowledged that while some of the changes in legislation and in court decisions on criminal responsibility are the result of the progress of psychiatric knowledge, some are also the result of the far more general change in the climate of opinion and the philosophy of the times. There is no question that psychiatric knowledge has greatly altered thinking in more fields of human experience than that of criminal respon-

---

[23] *The Mind of The Murderer*, pp. 119–23.

[24] See Hon. David L. Bazelon, "Mental Retardation: Some Legal and Moral Considerations," Address at the Presidential Session of the 1965 Annual Meetings of the American Orthopsychiatric Association, New York City:

On the whole, I think it is fair to say that judges and juries are increasingly achieving a degree of sophistication and concern which makes them ready to listen to more meaningful interpretations of human behavior. It is the expert witnesses who remain inhibited about telling in the courtroom what they learn in the clinic and hospital. Too often they testify to what they *think* the courts want to hear. They are obsessed, for instance, with the legal terminology in which the standard of responsibility is couched. Experts are not required to testify in terms of criminal responsibility. It is the function of court and jury to apply the test to the raw material supplied by the witnesses. But the raw material itself is too often lacking. I sometimes think that the psychologist and psychiatrist like to testify in terms of legal conclusions because they have nothing else to say.

sibility, yet it is this field that has attracted a disproportionate amount of attention from both law and psychiatry.

For over one hundred and twenty-five years the hot and cold wars between law and medicine and within the ranks of each discipline have continued as to how far mental illness or insanity may be used as a defense. The position of Dr. Isaac Ray that all old tests should be abolished and that in criminal cases insane persons should not be held responsible unless their acts are proved not to be the *direct* or *indirect* result of insanity has until recently stimulated as much writing and as little action as any other thesis ever proposed. Hailed by the American Psychiatric Association in 1864, Ray's belief has rarely been accepted by the courts in theory.[25] A study of cases reveals that regardless of the definition of insanity imposed by the statutes, they will usually be interpreted in such a way as to provide the legal language in which court and jury clothe the decision that seems just in the light of the evidence and of the emotions aroused by the offense among the jury members and in the community. The conviction of Jack Ruby for the murder of Lee Oswald is only one recent case in point. As one reads the story of the trial of Jack Ruby one is confronted by questionable trial practice, unbecoming judicial conduct, and the battle of the experts. Kaplan and Waltz[26] report that one witness presented issues in such a technical manner as to go beyond the competence of the jury. At the same time, counsel introduced such emotional overtones that the ability of the jury to listen objectively to medical experts was impaired. In describing the cross-examination of one distinguished expert by the District Attorney, the authors remark that "in deal-

[25] In testimony before the Royal Commission on Capital Punishment in England, Justice Felix Frankfurter is quoted as saying: "I think the M'Naghten Rules are very difficult for conscientious people and not difficult enough for people who say 'We'll just juggle them'" (Minutes of Evidence 26, Report 75, July 21, 1950 [London: H. M. Stationery Office, 1950], pp. 589–90).

[26] John Kaplan and Jon R. Waltz, *The Trial of Jack Ruby* (New York: Macmillan, 1965): "Experts with the most impeccable qualifications may honestly disagree over difficult and subtle questions just as lawyers and judges can and incessantly do differ as to the meaning of ambiguous statutes or court decisions" (p. 190). Dr. Guttmacher is reported to have said at a later time that the entire experience "was a most discouraging thing for a professional man" (p. 233). The cross-examination of Dr. Gibbs was on such a low level that its thrust was only to detract from his impressiveness (see pp. 298–303).

ing with Dr. Schaefer he orchestrated a symphony of whines, shouts and supercilious snarls."[27] Such conduct by the District Attorney struck responsive chords in the jury, which in turn reflected attitudes widely held in the community.

This trial provided the ultimate illustration of the extent to which our system of justice can be undermined when mere mortals see themselves, whether they be lawyers, members of the judiciary, or members of the jury, as the cynosure of all men's eyes.

This situation is sharply portrayed in the closing pages of *The Trial of Jack Ruby*, in which Ruby's conviction and death penalty are contrasted with the case of an Iowa man who stabbed his sixty-eight-year-old stepfather to death for cursing the assassinated President on Sunday, November 24, 1963. On a plea of guilty, the presiding judge referred to the assassination and stated that the entire nation was under stress and strain from the tragedy. He continued: "But that is not a reason for a citizen of the nation to release his emotions to the extent of causing another tragedy." The defendant was sentenced to eight years in prison and fined one thousand dollars. The judge then suspended the prison sentence and ended the hearing by wishing the defendant a Merry Christmas and a Happy New Year.

In the light of these two cases one cannot but wonder to what extent Ruby was offered up as a sacrifice on the altar of the guilty conscience of Dallas. One must ask to what extent members of the jury both wished they might kill the man who assassinated the President and feared this reaction, and then sought to wipe out their own guilt by imposing the extreme penalty on someone who had been held up to contempt and made to seem an alien in the community.

The criminal law, which has for centuries based its procedures on the determination of whether the proof establishes that the defendant committed the act *and* intended to do so, has been challenged repeatedly by questions as to the meaning of "intent." Judges, members of the jury, and the public have been beset by doubts as they develop a greater awareness of the dynamics of

[27] *Ibid.*, p. 204.

human conduct. The human or humanitarian revulsion against capital punishment of a person seen to be insane provided the opening wedge, followed by constant assaults on the legal doctrine of *mens rea* as based on free will. Attempts to bridge the chasm between that doctrine and concepts evolved by modern psychiatry have been a source of friction and non-communication. To expect a psychiatrist to speak in terms of whether a defendant's mental condition is such as to interfere with his acting "consciously and voluntarily" or with freedom of will assigns to him a non-scientific judgmental role far more relevant to religion than to science. It affronts the physician concerned with the whole person and the effect of pathology on his conduct, rather than with specific symptoms.

It is not only fear of the criminal but also a realistic awareness of society's limited ability to cope with the deviant personality that has caused the courts and the community to squirm and twist, to compromise, and to look for new ways of using without being controlled by the knowledge that the social sciences are presenting in ever greater volume.[28] The famous M'Naghten Rule, laid down in 1843,[29] has provided, despite all scientific battering at its doors, an edifice in which those who fear the intrusion of science in the field of law can take refuge. To these people new elements of uncertainty in the application of law or the diminution of fixed punishment appear to be a threat to law, as the sole agent of either retribution or deterrence.

Attempts to modify or expand the concept of mental illness beyond the ability "to know right from wrong" or to remove from the area of debate the issue of responsibility based on freedom of will led to a series of new formulas, including the "irresistible impulse" rule, which is based on the concept that disease can destroy will power and overwhelm cognitive capacity.[30] In 1951, in his dissenting opinion in *U. S. ex rel. Smith v. Beldi,*

---

[28] See *Longoria v. State*, 168 A.2d 695, 701 (Del. 1961); *State v. Davies,* 148 A.2d 251 (Conn. 1959).

[29] *David M'Naghten's Case*, 10 C & F 200, 8 English Reports 718 (1843).

[30] *Parsons v. State*, 81 Ala. 577, 2 So. 854 (1886). By 1957, fifteen states, the federal courts, and the military had all coupled this test with the M'Naghten Rule in one way or another (see the American Bar Foundation study, *The Mentally Disabled and the Law*, p. 332).

Judge Biggs stated that "changes can be effected and reason can be brought to the law of criminal insanity."[31] Finally, in 1954, the opinion in the Durham case reduced the requirement of proof, or enlarged the legal definition of the insanity defense to include criminal acts shown to be the "product of the disease."[32] Judge Bazelon, in a significant opinion, wrote that "existing tests of criminal responsibility are obsolete and should be superseded."

Despite almost unanimous acclaim by psychiatrists and wide discussion in the 1950's, like Dr. Ray's thesis a century earlier, the formula of Judge Bazelon has not been generally accepted, nor has it succeeded in overcoming the fears and doubts that continue to prevail.[33] In discussing the Durham decision, Dr. Philip Roche pointed out that our jurisprudence, like our traditional child-rearing, is based on the abstract notion that if an adult or child who knows better does wrong, he is responsible and punishable.[34] Dr. Roche deplores the energy wasted in disputes over verbal abstractions in the process of assigning guilt and welcomes the Durham opinion as one that imposes "on lawyers and physicians alike the pain of facing the facts of surrounding reality and remove[s] the barriers to communications between the professions." He warns, however, that behavior and mental illness are not separable and that one cannot properly say that mental illness causes one to commit a crime. Rather, criminality and mental illness must be seen as processes "reflecting the breakdown of psychic controls and the release of latent antisocial drives common to all." These processes he describes as manifestations of rebellion directed outwardly or inwardly and demonstrating in different ways regressive withdrawal from surrounding reality.[35]

---

[31] 192 F.2d 540 (C.A.3d 1951).

[32] *Durham* v. *U.S.*, 214 F.2d 862 (D.C. Cir. 1954).

[33] The M'Naghten Rule is being applied either alone or in connection with other tests of criminal responsibility within the federal jurisdiction, the armed forces, and in all of the states except Vermont, New Hampshire, and perhaps Montana (see American Bar Foundation, *The Mentally Disabled and the Law*, p. 332n).

[34] Philip Q. Roche, M.D., "Criminality and Mental Illness—Two Faces of the Same Coin," *University of Chicago Law Review*, XXII, No. 2 (Winter, 1955), 320ff.

[35] *Ibid.*, p. 323.

The Durham decision was hailed as the first official break-through in the area of criminal responsibility by Dr. Manfred S. Guttmacher, who noted that in recent polls of the American Psychiatric Association and of the Group for the Advancement of Psychiatry, the M'Naghten Rule was overwhelmingly rejected. He also noted that even before 1843, when it was enunciated, Dr. Ray had criticized the criterion of responsibility based on an ability to distinguish between right and wrong.[36] However, Dr. Guttmacher also anticipated persistent difficulties since there could be no exact measurements of human behavior and there would continue to be uncertainty and differences of opinion as to what constitutes "a diseased or defective mental condition, and questions as to whether a specific act was the product of the mental abnormality." He saw the chief merit of the new rule as its permitting the psychiatrist "to present his testimony in regard to the mental condition of the accused in concepts that are familiar to him and that actually exist in mental life."[37]

Dr. Gregory Zilboorg hailed Durham as finally disposing of the traditional right-and-wrong test and described the M'Naghten Rule as a "strange left-over of ancient prejudice couched in legalistic terms and meaning so little." He pointed out that "it is only with regard to mental disease in a criminal case that the law assumes to dictate its formalistic views to medicine."[38] While seeing the *Durham* decision as one of historic significance, Dr. Zilboorg still raised questions as to how lower courts and counsel would apply it and how psychiatrists, heirs to generations of forensic psychiatry, would respond—whether they would be willing to stick to the "clinical grindstone" and not trespass in the field of law.

In sharp contrast to the thinking of Judge Bazelon and leaders of psychiatric thought, Professor Herbert Wechsler has ex-

---

[36] "The Psychiatrist as an Expert," in *ibid.*, pp. 325–30.

[37] *Ibid.*, p. 329. In a dissenting opinion, Judge Van Voorhis, after quoting from testimony, described the psychiatrist as being "in an impossible position —sworn to tell the whole truth and prevented by the court from telling it" (*People* v. *Horton*, 308 N.Y. 1, 20–21, 123 N.E.2d 609, 618–19 [1954]). See also Henry Weihofen, "The Flowering of New Hampshire," *University of Chicago Law Review*, XXII, No. 2 (Winter, 1955), 356–66.

[38] "A Step toward Enlightened Justice," in *ibid.*, pp. 331–35.

pressed his firm belief that the category of "irresponsible" must be defined in terms

> so extreme that to the ordinary man, burdened by passion and beset by large temptations, the exculpation of the irresponsibles bespeaks no weakness in law. . . . It is public justice which, in the interest of the common good, prescribes a standard all must strive to satisfy who can, those whose nature or nurture leads them to conform with difficulty no less than those who find compliance easy.[39]

To Professor Wechsler the essence of the issue raised by the Durham case is the question of whether we are ready to hold that something less than a total impairment or incapacity of mental condition is to be regarded as relevant to the question of responsibility.[40] This position was expressed in the decision in *Fisher* v. *United States*, which affirmed the first-degree murder conviction of a defendant who was described as an aggressive psychopath with low emotional response and borderline mental deficiency. In the opinion, Judge Thurman Arnold wrote: "In the determination of guilt, age-old conceptions of individual moral responsibility cannot be abandoned without creating a laxity of enforcement that undermines the whole administration of criminal law."[41]

Despite the heavy dosage of psychiatric material and jargon in our novels, magazine articles, and even newspapers, one must question whether there is any deep understanding among a large segment of our society, including both learned professors and judges. One of the harshest critics of the decision in the Durham case, Edward de Grazia, centered much of his attack on those who naively assumed that the defendant found not guilty by reason of insanity has more to look forward to than the defendant

[39] Herbert Wechsler, "The Criteria of Criminal Responsibility," in *ibid.*, pp. 374–75.

[40] *Ibid.*, p. 376.

[41] 149 F.2d 28, 29 (App. D.C. 1945). This statement was cited with approval as recently as 1961 in *Dusky* v. *United States* (295 F.2d 743, 753–54, 8th Cir. [1961]). The position seems astounding, since the statutes in nearly all states specify the institutions to which the criminally insane or those acquitted for insanity shall be assigned (see American Bar Foundation, *The Mentally Disabled and the Law*, p. 353).

found guilty. He spoke of the efforts to distinguish the "mad from the bad" as a Pyrrhic victory so long as the mad are treated as badly as the bad.[42]

The instinctive or reflex demands for retributive and excessive punishment when a vicious crime is committed that involves sexual deviance, narcotics addiction, or multiple offenses has led to ill-considered legislative and statutory punishments that are in conflict with all knowledge from the field of social science.[43] Elaborate efforts to reduce punishment when mental illness is found reflect our contradictory attitudes toward the mentally ill. In these efforts one finds both fear and distaste. One finds elements of sympathy. One also finds a lack of readiness to re-examine the meaning of mental illness, its effect on the individual defendant, and the treatment he requires. The persistence of prison sentences rather than mandatory hospitalization for the mentally ill mocks the "humanity" of such efforts. Their inherent contradictions are illustrated by the position of the American Bar Foundation: "The defense of partial responsibility should be available to defendants, but the reduced prison confinement should be followed by a period of indeterminate hospitalization when necessary for the public safety."[44] In other words, first let us punish and deny treatment to the mentally ill, thus probably making their condition worse, if not hopeless, and then let us hospitalize them indefinitely to safeguard the community! Rigid safeguards for discharge from the hospital to the community have been set up by statute. At times they have been so rigid as to bar release to a civil hospital even after the expiration of the maximum sentence which could have been imposed on the mentally ill defendant if he had been found guilty. In North Caro-

---

[42] "The Distinction of Being Mad," *University of Chicago Law Review,* XXII, No. 2 (Winter, 1955), 339–55.

[43] Judge Biggs expressed the fear that the majority of citizens today would agree with Sir James Fitzjames Stephen, who wrote in 1883: "I think it highly desirable that criminals should be hated, that the punishments inflicted upon them should be so contrived as to give expression to that hatred. . . . Judge Biggs also deplored the unwillingness of judges today to avail themselves freely of the services of psychiatrists (*The Guilty Mind,* p. 174n).

[44] *The Mentally Disabled and the Law,* p. 367.

lina, for example, if a capital crime is involved, discharge from hospitalization requires a special act of the state legislature.[45]

In view of the incidence of criminal recidivism where there is no defense of insanity, the precautions taken to protect the community against the defendant who was mentally ill when he committed an offense appear extreme. They may represent society's pathological fear or dislike of a person who is presented as combining two characteristics repellant to the community: criminality and mental illness. The reflexes of counteraggression found in legal circles as well as in the general community are reinforced by the failure to implement even the comparatively small and often disjointed legislative efforts to authorize treatment and rehabilitation of the "criminal." Surely the time has come to place less emphasis on definitions in the law and more emphasis on what happens to defendants after conviction. The necessity for capital punishment has been extensively challenged.[46] Imprisonment instead of treatment for narcotics addicts has been seriously criticized. Conviction and imprisonment of the chronic alcoholic has been challenged.[47] New attitudes toward the treatment of deviant sexual behavior between consenting adults have emerged in England, at international conferences, and even in the United States. The provision of outside work opportunities for prisoners believed ready for return to the community has been proposed by the Attorney General of the United States.

Each of these positions, proposed by knowledgeable people and opposed as threats to law and order in our society, has its basis in new knowledge about why people act in certain ways, the waste resulting from past forms of punishment, and the hope of more effective forms of treatment. They also are based in large part on a growing concern for the individuals who have

[45] *Ibid.*, pp. 353–54.

[46] See Henry Weihofen, *The Urge to Punish* (New York: Farrar, Straus & Cudahy, 1956), p. 156: "Psychiatrists have paid relatively little attention to the validity or fallacy of the 'deterrent' effect of the death penalty, and have largely been content to leave such investigations to the sociologists and penal reformers."

[47] See *Easter* v. *District of Columbia*, 361 F.2d 50 (D.C. Cir. 1966). For discussion, see Chapter II below.

emerged from the mass, become visible, and therefore command more concern as human beings. With the relegation of the debate over "free will" versus "determinism" to the antiquarians, the far more difficult task of applying new knowledge in the administration of criminal justice can be begun in earnest.

One cause for the delay in applying the new knowledge must be laid at the doorstep of the social scientists themselves. They have not made clear the difference between diagnostics and treatment. They have not exposed sham treatment. They have not insisted that without preparation for the use of increasing freedom the prisoner will be incapable of or at least unlikely to escape further involvement in criminal action. The tough task of actually working with criminals in prison, with the mentally ill in prison hospitals, and with the problem-burdened families of which they are a part and to which they will return has been all too often avoided.

A second serious barrier to a reasonable approach to the problem of criminal responsibility is the acceptance of the theory that while medicine must recognize the wide spectrum of mental health and mental illness, the law must act on the basis of clear lines of demarcation between them.[48] It is argued that not to have such a clear distinction not only violates the traditional right (often theoretical) of the criminal to know (often theoretical) what the consequences of his act will be, but also places an unbearable burden on those who must exercise the authority of law.

It is significant that in the American Bar Foundation study the authors, in commenting on the Durham rule, wrote:

> The difficulty with such a situation [equating criminal irresponsibility with mental disease] is that criminal laws thus far have been administered on the basis of a fixed standard, equally applicable to all persons. The attempt to individualize justice through

---

[48] See Weihofen, *The Urge to Punish*: there is "no clear dichotomy between mental health, and mental illness. The one shades by degrees into the other, and the law . . . must of necessity draw a line demarking the degree or form of mental illness or the effects produced thereby that will serve to render a person mentally irresponsible" (p. 2).

the treatment or punishment of persons on a case by case basis is antithetical to our present concepts of administering justice.[49]

While this rigid, impersonal, and ivory-tower approach to criminal justice is in conflict with other attitudes expressed in the study, in this section the authors go on to assert that "the problem of discriminating between those individuals for whom a 'punitive-correctional' disposition is appropriate and those who should be subjected to a 'medical-custodial' disposition is essentially a legal question." Nevertheless, the study states dogmatically that the question is one of ethics, morals, and social policy, and that there is thus no *a priori* reason why the law should absolve all persons suffering mental disease from criminal responsibility and punishment.[50] With the question of how the mentally ill should be treated in our society at this time in the light of modern knowledge thus reduced to one of *a priori* reasons, the real issues can be and are avoided.

One may quarrel with the M'Naghten Rule as putting all the emphasis on the cognitive capacity of the defendant, or one may agree with Judge Bazelon that the courts have erred in failing to interpret "know" to mean more than the cognitive process.[51] One may deplore the tardy recognition of the role played by the emotions and the unconscious in determinations of mental health or mental illness. In the end, however, the question goes back not only to differences in the training and knowledge of the individuals but to far deeper feelings and anxieties that have long prevented change in many aspects of criminal law itself and in its administration: "Our unconscious helps explain not only why criminals behave as they do, but also why the best of us behave as we do toward criminals. Our righteous indignation against wrongdoers is more often than we unconsciously realize an expression of our own strong but repressed aggressive impulses."[52]

Society is fearful of recognizing the extent to which such aggressions exist within it. In an earlier Isaac Ray lecture, Dr.

---

[49] *The Mentally Disabled and the Law*, p. 343n.
[50] *Ibid.*, p. 343.
[51] Judge David Bazelon, "Equal Justice for the Unequal," The Isaac Ray Award Lectures, 1961 (mimeographed).
[52] Weihofen, *The Urge to Punish*, p. 13n.

Philip Roche tackled the question of "to what extent can a system of criminal justice based on metaphysical concepts of moral responsibility . . . be replaced, in part or wholly, by a system based upon the operational philosophy of contemporary science. It is important to make some estimate of the tolerable limits of such a change." He also warned that it was necessary "for psychiatrists to reexamine their own premises and determine to what extent their operations are useful or valid in matters of adjudicating criminal responsibility."[53] The law will be resistant to scientific teachings concerning the mind of man until those teachings can be transformed into services, rehabilitation, or preventive work that will minimize mental illness and demonstrate that the punishment of former ages can be replaced by more effective measures. Dr. Roche suggested four areas in which psychiatry could have a role other than in the trial itself: (1) advising on the question of the triability of the defendant; (2) giving information and advice on the appropriate disposition of the convicted criminal; (3) providing techniques for developing the self-awareness and contributing to the reform of the convicted criminal; (4) advising on questions connected with his release from custody.[54]

While psychiatric involvement in these four areas would represent marked progress in the administration of criminal justice, Dr. Roche's emphasis on the psychiatrist's role as technical adviser reflects the extent to which psychiatry is both prepared and unprepared to meet the need for far more direct service. Chief Justice Weintraub has also expressed the honest concern of those held responsible for the administration of justice:

> No one will dispute that society must be protected from the insane as well as the sane. The area of disagreement is whether a civil or criminal process should be employed when forbidden acts have been committed. If we could think of a conviction as a finding

[53] Roche, "Criminality and Mental Illness," p. 248n.

[54] In thirty-four states the determination of the issue of whether a defendant is capable of standing trial must be made by the judge, "but frequently he is authorized to employ experts. In at least 39 jurisdictions, hospitalization is made mandatory when the defendant is adjudged incapable of standing trial or being sentenced" (American Bar Foundation, *The Mentally Disabled and the Law*, p. 361n).

that the mortal in question has demonstrated his capacity for anti-social conduct, most of the battle would be decided. What would remain is the employment of such post-conviction techniques as would redeem the offender if he can be redeemed and secure him if he cannot.[55]

Despite this reasoned position, Judge Weintraub may be far too sanguine about a wall that persistently prevents the application of new knowledge by both criminal and civil courts. This wall has three buttresses which reinforce one another in resisting change.

The first buttress is the false complacency of the community, which believes the protestations of those entrusted with new services who, despite their inability to fulfill their responsibilities, assert that such services are actually being provided. The pretense is made that psychiatric treatment is being given in both public and voluntary institutions, when in fact only occasional diagnostic examinations are available. The pretense is made that work is being done to strengthen a family in preparation for the return of a child or an adult offender, when in fact only an untrained person has been sent out to make an examination of the physical conditions of the home before release of the offender. The pretense is made that probation or parole services are being rendered to rehabilitate released criminals, when in fact reporting centers are manned by overworked and underskilled people who can only allot a few moments to each person on their case load. The pretense is made that the courts mete out justice, when in fact the meat-grinder conveyor-belt system of justice in our lower courts rarely allows the individuality of the defendant to become visible. The second and interrelated buttress against change is the lack of well-trained clinicians to provide the services needed by troubled individuals. The third and strongest buttress is the community attitude or non-attitude toward the individual who troubles it and does not conform to its rules. In the words of Warren P. Hill, folklore will not be exchanged for reality as long as a system of criminal law breeding "only waste, cruelty, and more crime . . . continues to be harmonious with the other practices of

---

[55] *State* v. *Lucas*, 152 A.2d 50, 75 (N.J. 1959).

living. . . . the growth of our social conscience has been so slight as to be presently incapable of sustaining ambitious programs of community social planning. . . . we cling to the punitive system of control as a distraction from the disturbing realities."[56]

---

[56] "The Psychological Realism of Thurman Arnold," *University of Chicago Law Review*, XXII, No. 2 (Winter, 1955), 377, 396.

Chapter II

THE CHANGING, ROLE OF LAW

Law, its potential and its practice, means many things to many people today, as it has throughout the ages. To many it still represents only the restrictions on what we may do and the formal threat of punishment if we disobey it. To others it means the technical, purchasable skills through which property interests can best be protected and advanced. To still others, it means far more—a social institution both burdened and strengthened by traditions, yet capable of change, to achieve better ways of living while providing for the maximum of freedom and equality for every individual within society.

The rule of law in the lives of men has varied vastly in different societies and at different times. What it means to those who have the power to control a society and what it means to those subject to such power provides a fair barometer of effective human values at any given time and place. In the writings of Justice Cardozo one finds the legal scholar challenged by the moral imperative to find ways in which he can do justice creatively without doing violence to the rule of law:

> What we are seeking is not merely the justice that one receives when his rights and duties are determined by the law as it is; what we are seeking is the justice to which law in its making should conform. . . .
>
> The Judge interprets the social conscience and gives effect to it in law, but in so doing he helps to form and modify the conscience he interprets. Discovery and creation react upon each other.[1]

[1] Benjamin N. Cardozo, *The Growth of the Law* (New Haven, Conn.: Yale University Press, 1924), pp. 87, 96–97.

The achievements of judges in the early part of this century may seem but slight adventures in the development of judge-made law to protect the rights of men in a democratic society. However, the seeds of the great trees that have since grown tall were planted in those days. Before the Depression and the New Deal those who sought to interpret law so as to achieve greater justice saw the decisions of the courts as the main vehicle for progress. They did not foresee the major role that the legislative branch of our government would play in changing the rule of law.[2] When new problems arose, even liberal judges saw justice within a framework consistent with symmetry and order. They did not see that the rule of law would have to be enlarged by legislation as well as by judicial decision in order that old problems might be tackled in new ways. They did not foresee the role that the social sciences would have to play in the development of law as enacted by our legislative bodies, as interpreted by our courts, and as implemented by ever-growing administrative bodies.

In no area, not even in that of property rights, have those responsible for developing new legal concepts been more timid than where such concepts and resulting action affect what is regarded as the imponderable, unknown, and fearsome world of man's psyche. Here the notions of the devil and the witch's brew, combined with superstition, religious traditions, and fixed concepts of personal responsibility, reinforced the reluctance to look at men and their problems in the light of the new science of mental health. Physical medicine has had an easier time. Seen as boon rather than bane to those whose lives it touched, it has generally been regarded by law with almost unquestioning obeisance. Psychiatry has had a far harder row to hoe. First concerned with the control or "care" of the insane, it has for over half a century been moving forward into a world of the unknown, the inner

[2] *Ibid.*, p. 134: "Legislation can eradicate a cancer, right some hoary wrong, correct some definitely established evil, which defies the feeble remedies, the distinctions and the fictions, familiar to the judicial progress. Legislation, too, can sum up at times and simplify the conclusions reached by courts, and give them new validity. Even then its relief is provisional and temporary." See also Archibald Cox, "The Supreme Court, 1965 Term," *Harvard Law Review*, LXXX, No. 1 (November, 1966), 91–122.

world of man. As physicians moved beyond physical manifestations of mental illness and began to wrestle with the causes, they embarked on a voyage whose destination was the freeing of man from those inner restrictions and experiences that kept him from functioning fully. Such a goal has far more in common with the aspirations of those who see law as an instrument of society to enlarge the freedom of men than is often recognized. The early concern with law and penal institutions as they affected the insane gave way to a period in which the young science of psychiatry concentrated on the study of the causes of mental illness or disturbances, and on new methods of treatment for the individual patient.

Law was long perceived largely as a negative restraining force rather than as a positive instrument for modifying institutional patterns in society.[3] It is only in recent years that psychiatry has begun to view law as a social institution that must be understood and modified if new concepts for treatment are to be made widely available, and if preventive mental health services are to be established. The psychiatrist, while working on the development of the science of mental health, felt alienated and alien from the law as a significant social institution. In turn, men of law in legislatures and courts regarded psychiatry as not only alien and suspect but as profoundly threatening.[4]

---

[3] See Gilbert Geis, "Sociology and Sociological Jurisprudence, Adventure of Lore and Law," *Kentucky Law Journal*, LII, No. 2 (1964), 279. Geis describes the condescending attitude of sociologists toward the law, which they saw as a static and anachronistic system whose members were generally reluctant to accept the sociological position of the time as meaningful. See also Geis, p. 286, quoting James Landis (*Social Control*, pp. 444–45): "For the most part, the law has been punitive in its attitude and involved only with questions of interpreting statutes, not with questions of human relationships. . . ."

[4] "Historically, legislatures and courts have not had much assistance from medical science in accomplishing the twin objectives of the law: the preservation of the maximum rights and liberties of the mentally disabled and the maintenance of the physical welfare of the patient and the community" (American Bar Foundation, *The Mentally Disabled and the Law*, p. 3). One must question whether this is a fair charge and whether one can thus assign blame. Legislatures have not met medical needs. When Senator Kennedy made serious charges about the inadequate care and treatment of the mentally retarded in New York State institutions in August, 1966, it was disclosed that despite requests from the State Medical Director, which were supported by the Governor, the Legislature had cut proposed additional budgetary grants from $100 million to $30 million.

A significant factor in building the new relationship between law and psychiatry has been the steady incorporation or assimilation in wider and wider circles of segments of the knowledge derived from mental health.[5] Another essential ingredient is the changing role of law in our society as legislatures, administrative agencies, and the judiciary are confronted with the need to correct old injustices and to provide new ways in which the problems of people in our society can be dealt with more effectively. Finally, as the mental health of more and more people has become a major community concern, government agencies have reached out to psychiatry for help and, in turn, have presented to psychiatry a challenge of dimensions few psychiatrists had anticipated.

Limiting the usefulness of psychiatry to questions of mental illness or mental responsibility is a thing of the past. Its value in many areas has been recognized, though often under various rubrics and in fragmented fashion. Its impact can be noted in the use of probation, the development of parole, the sentencing of prisoners, and the establishment of rehabilitation centers and residential treatment institutions. Its work is reflected in the organization of social courts and in legislation dealing with certain offenders, including narcotics addicts, alcoholics, sexual psychopaths, delinquents, and youthful offenders. Its influence is echoed in the changing attitudes expressed by legislators and judges as they face health, housing, welfare, and educational problems in the community.

At present there is an urgent need to move from the haphazard, fragmented use of mental health concepts and knowledge to their integration into the planning for legislation and its implementation by the social institutions, including the courts, which determine how such services will be used. Today we are living in an age different from all others insofar as the rule of law is concerned. Legislation enacted by federal, state, and local bodies and judicial decisions, instead of lagging behind the

---

[5] See C. Vann Woodward, "Even Luther Is on the Couch," *New York Times Book Review*, January 24, 1965. Professor Woodward expects that sooner or later most historians will be touched in one way or another by the work of social scientists: "They will be using new concepts and vocabulary without necessarily being aware of the origins of either, any more than they are conscious of their debt to theology or metaphysics for older concepts and vocabulary."

thinking and action of the community, has in recent years led the procession. The creative genius of the authors of the Constitution has been rediscovered and is seen to permit the translation of its high purposes into the laws and life of the American people.[6]

It was in this spirit that the Supreme Court in 1954 reversed or overruled the earlier acceptance of tradition, customs, and rules of law that directed or permitted the segregation of school children on the basis of race. The Court noted the absence of public education at the time of the adoption of the Fourteenth Amendment. It found that only by considering public education in the light of its present place in the nation could it "be determined whether segregation in public schools deprived the plaintiffs of equal protection of the laws":[7]

> Today, education is perhaps the most important function of state and local governments. . . . It is doubtful that any child may reasonably be expected to succeed in life if he is denied the opportunity of an education. Such an opportunity, where the State has undertaken to provide it, is a right which must be made available to all on equal terms.[7]

This approach to the rule of law in contemporary life has invited fuller utilization of the social sciences and of mental health precepts and practices in many new areas. It has provided new goals. It has also led to dangerous complacency and false pride in our achievements, since neither laws nor court decisions necessarily create new attitudes, the administrative machinery, the money, or the personnel needed to make them meaningful. There is the all too common assumption that when a good law is enacted or a great decision is rendered directed to the improvement of public welfare, the task is done. Such laws and decisions only lay the foundation and provide the opportunity for constructive social action. The major tasks still lie ahead.[8] What

[6] See Norman Dorsen, "Civil Liberty under a Constitutional Document," *The Record of the Association of the Bar of the City of New York* (February, 1966).

[7] *Brown v. Board of Education*, 347 U.S. 483, 493 (1954).

[8] Southern Regional Council, *School Desegregation 1966: The Slow Undoing* (Atlanta, Ga., December, 1966): "A decade of litigation over the 1954 school decision of the Supreme Court had in September, 1966, resulted in a pitifully small amount of desegregation. Approximately two per cent of the 2,896,000 Negro children in the eleven Southern states were in desegregated schools in 1964–1965" (p. 4).

man learns, what science discovers, inevitably become part of the institutions of the society in which he lives. The pace at which this occurs in turn determines what is later seen as the rate of progress.

It was only as new frontiers disappeared, as the number of first-generation Americans diminished, as our population changed from an agricultural to an increasingly urban one, as the Depression struck at those who had not previously been poor, as workers and unemployed organized, and as technology imposed the need for more education that the necessity for imposing new obligations and providing new opportunities through law was slowly recognized. The concept of law in a modern society had to evolve into one embracing concern for the welfare of the individual as well as for the protection of society against the criminal and the protection of property.

In the last thirty years we have witnessed the steady proliferation of state and federal laws to conserve natural resources, to provide social security, to control media of communication, to provide public health services, to encourage education, to assure minimum wages, to support the farmer in various ways, to provide more adequate housing, to subsidize medical and social research, to develop mental health services, and to outlaw discrimination against people on the basis of race, creed, or color.

The extent to which those who continue to develop law in legislative halls, in administrative agencies, or in the courts will effectively meet society's needs will depend in large part on the growth of knowledge in the social sciences and the development of the methods and means by which such knowledge is made relevant and useful to the lawmakers. As law expands to touch the lives of ever more people, the science of mental health will be challenged to provide one of the most essential ingredients for meeting the needs of a healthy society.

In the thrust to meet the needs of people in our complex society, we have turned increasingly to legislation as the instrument through which to accomplish new objectives. The proliferation of legislation on federal, state, and local levels to raise wage standards, to end discriminatory practices, and to provide health, welfare, and educational benefits provides the most obvious example. The Civil Rights Acts of 1964 and 1965, the Elementary and Secondary Education Act of 1965, and the Economic Opportunity Act of 1964 were directed not only toward the correction of old injustices and inequalities. Clearly, they were also aimed at discovering and providing ways through which greater equality of opportunity would be accorded to individuals.

In a summary of federal legislation affecting social welfare, over the past five years one finds a growing acceptance of governmental responsibility under law for programs directed to both the physical and mental health of millions of people in this country.[9] In the area of health, the spectrum of legislation enacted during this short period extended from air pollution to the training of nurses and advancing of loans to students, from research on water resources to maternal and child health and mental retardation, from vaccination assistance to construction of community health centers. In education, the legislation reached from provision of library services and practical nurse training, through manpower development and training, to the Higher Educational Facilities Act of 1963. In welfare, public welfare amendments legislation included provisions for tackling such problems as juvenile delinquency, youth offenses, and foster care for dependent children.

Within recent years state legislators have had to vote on new procedures and methods for treating delinquent children and youths, the mentally ill, the mentally defective, the narcotics addict, the alcoholic, the sex offender, the deprived preschool child, and the child who is "not motivated" to learn. While legislators will listen with open minds, one hopes, to differing points of view on all the problems on which they must act, it cannot be expected that they will be experts in such diverse fields. Yet they cannot

---

[9] U.S., Department of Health, Education, and Welfare. *Major Federal Legislation Affecting Social Welfare, 1961–1965* (Washington, D.C.: Government Printing Office, 1965). The reference material relating to social change through social welfare and law might equally well have been compiled to show the extent to which law is becoming an increasingly significant vehicle in the planning and provision of services for the health and welfare of individuals.

abdicate their responsibility, as legislators, to hear the evidence and then make their decisions.

The fullest disclosure of differences within the field of mental health and in the social sciences provides the best safeguard against errors. In science, as in law, there are selfless men and self-seekers, pioneers and fad-makers, independent workers and bandwagon followers. Legislators must beware lest they swallow whole whatever bait is cast upon the sea of social problems without regard to the identity of the fisherman or for what he fishes. So too, the agencies that are entrusted with administering new laws must avoid being captivated by flashy applications or "grantsmanship" which bear little promise of attaining the goals desired by the legislators. As one foreign scientist remarked, there would be the greatest cutback in history in the total number of sociologists if non-essential research, focused on repetitive detail, were subjected to a deflationary period.

Legislators have the responsibility for determining how public funds are to be spent for services to meet new social goals. They are understandably reluctant to transfer great power from the courts to social scientists, physicians, or psychiatrists without evidence that these men are both able and willing to provide such services and that the constitutional rights of those served will not be denied or overlooked.

Both law and psychiatry are caught up in the demand that they should prevent persons from behaving in such a way as to disturb the peace of the community, or at least control and rehabilitate them. There have been centuries when law continued to assert its omnipotence in achieving this purpose, despite all evidence to the contrary. In recent years the statements of some psychiatrists as to how antisocial conduct can best be controlled have seemed to reflect delusions of omniscience. Other psychiatrists have not only appeared disinterested in the vast problems of the lawbreaker, but have disclaimed the skills with which to combat the problems he presents. Debates within both professions and between individual members of each profession continue, and the fires of controversy are fueled not only by members of the professions but by the insistent demands of the community for effective help.

Despite resistance from some quarters, a little knowledge of mental health, an increasing awareness that harsh punishment has not proved effective, and an attempt to blend modern science with traditional controls continue to infuse new laws with strange admixtures and even contradictory dosages of law and medicine. At a Senate Judiciary Sub-Committee hearing the distinguished former Director of the Federal Bureau of Prisons, James V. Bennett, pressed for "seed money for developing or trying out a system of civil penalties or clinic treatment for offenses involving some social maladjustment, alcoholism, or drug addiction" and expressed dissatisfaction with present methods of dealing with such problems: "Our trial courts, particularly the minor courts, have been inundated by a massive increase in the number of criminal cases. Untold thousands of alcoholics, juvenile delinquents, drug addicts, mentally ill persons, social misfits are now being disposed of on an assembly line basis."[10]

While psychiatrists may not appreciate the equation of therapy and penalties, the traditional belief that treatment cannot be given in an authoritarian setting has been slowly modified, like many other dogma, in the face of significant experiments in certain courts and other authoritarian environments. The legislation enacted in many fields reflects compromises between those forces bent on protecting the community against deviant behavior and those which recognize the need for preventive action in the community and for services for individuals whose rehabilitation depends on treatment. Compromises and even contradictory positions are to be found in the legislation affecting criminal responsibility and the treatment of narcotics addicts, alcoholics, and the mentally ill.

In 1965 the federal government entered the correctional field in a new way when Congress enacted legislation for a study leading to an action program at the state, interstate, and national levels.[11] This legislation was directed toward raising the num-

[10] *New York Times*, July 23, 1965, p. 31.

[11] U.S., Congress, *The Correctional Rehabilitation Study Act of 1965*, H.R. 2263; signed by President Johnson on September 10, 1965.

ber and quality of correctional personnel. In supporting the measure, one congressman, noting that the cost of crime totaled $27 billion each year, stated that "it is economically unsound and also inhuman to forget these people. There must be enough skilled rehabilitation and prevention personnel to put into practice research findings on crime and delinquency and to develop the potentialities of offenders."[12]

In July, 1965, President Johnson also announced the establishment of the President's Commission on Law Enforcement and Administration of Justice, set up to investigate the causes of crime, the adequacy of law enforcement machinery, and "the factors encouraging respect or disrespect for law" at national, state, and local levels. It was Attorney General Katzenbach who questioned many traditional legal procedures in his appearance before a congressional committee in 1965. He noted that "of the approximately six million arrests in the United States in 1964, fully one-third were for drunkenness. . . . Better ways to handle drunks than tossing them in jail should be considered. . . . Similarly, drug addiction and . . . offenses arising out of family disputes or landlord tenant differences could be removed from the criminal process."[13]

The federal government has now enacted legislation that would give the Bureau of Prisons authority to establish work programs and halfway houses. Success with such legislation had been reported by several states. The Prisoner Rehabilitation Act of 1965,[14] unanimously approved by both houses of Congress, contains three major provisions: (1) it authorizes the Attorney General of the United States to commit or transfer prisoners to residential community treatment centers or halfway houses; (2) it authorizes the Attorney General to grant furloughs from prison of up to thirty days for personal reasons (such as illness or death of a member of the prisoner's family) or for purposes related to release; (3) finally, it permits prisoners to obtain

---

[12] Representative Edith Green, Oregon, Address to 12th National Institute on Crime and Delinquency, *National Council on Crime and Delinquency (NCCD) News*, XLIV, No. 4 (September–October, 1965).

[13] Quoted in *ibid.*, p. 2.

[14] U.S., *Public Laws*, 89–176.

private employment and to participate in programs of community training while continuing as inmates in the penal institutions to which they have been committed. Among the interesting features of the law is one that authorizes the commitment of an offender to a community center at any time during his sentence, even directly from court.[15]

Among the debaters on correctional legislation one still finds persons to whom punishment and retribution provide the only correctional answer. Thus, prior to the hearings on the Prisoner Rehabilitation Act of 1965, J. Edgar Hoover criticized the high rate of recidivism of persons on probation, suspended sentence, parole, or conditional release. He referred to all such procedures as "leniency" and gave figures designed to frighten people into opposition to the expansion of such measures. He gave no figures on the recidivism rate of those who were denied such "leniency." As one read his statement, the unspoken premise seemed to be that if every person who committed an offense were immediately jailed, convicted, sentenced, and held in prison the maximum term, no offenses would be committed (at least while the defendant was in prison), and that the percentage of recidivists would thus be lowered. No concern was indicated for the price that would be exacted from the defendant, his family, or the community by such a Draconian application of "the law." No regard was paid to the earlier failures of this punitive application of law or to the promise of rehabilitation through methods concerned with the potential functioning of the individual.

---

[15] In Israel prisoners are entitled to an appropriate wage for work done, of which a small part is paid in cash and the remainder put aside for use upon release. Every prisoner may be granted, at the discretion of the prison authorities, home leave not exceeding ninety-six hours, and the privilege is widely used where there is a reasonable expectation that the prisoner will not commit further offenses. This procedure is reported to have raised the morale of prisoners, and there have been almost no violations of such leaves. See Haim H. Cohen, *Legislation and Judicial Process in the Field of Criminal Law* (State of Israel Report, the Prevention of Crime and the Treatment of Offenders in Israel; Jerusalem: State of Israel, 1965), p. 20. See also *Laws of New York* (1965), c. 522, amending sec. 454 of the Family Court Act to authorize granting of permission for a respondent to go to work during a commitment for willful non-compliance with a support order.

In contrast to this approach, the Attorney General of the United States supported legislation to authorize creation of "half-way houses" for older prisoners so that they might be paroled to work and earn some money before they were released. He also supported emergency or rehabilitation leaves from prison and the enlargement of the work release programs.[16]

These contradictory approaches toward correctional legislation by the head of the F.B.I. and the Attorney General illustrate the contradictory positions presented to legislative bodies on the exclusion or inclusion of consideration of the mental health of the individual and the knowledge of the social sciences in modifying old practices. It is therefore not surprising that legislation should frequently reflect both the recognition of the need for more humane and constructive use of law and concern lest change expose the "law-abiding community" to additional hazards from "criminal elements." Indeed, Senator Edward V. Long, while supporting the Prisoner Rehabilitation Act, also promised that the exercise of authority granted under the Act would be used conservatively, that there would be virtually no risk to citizens and property, that no costs to the government were in-

---

[16] Evidence was presented at the congressional hearings by the Federal Bureau of Prisons and by the State of North Carolina in support of the effectiveness of work release programs, jobs for prisoners on release, and halfway houses.

In July, 1965, Attorney General Katzenbach urged that Congress do away with the death penalty in the federal courts, thus placing himself in opposition to J. Edgar Hoover, who has traditionally insisted on its retention. The statement of the Attorney General followed a report by the Bureau of Prisons on executions from 1930 to 1963, published in 1964. The report noted that while capital punishment might still be legally imposed in forty-four civil jurisdictions (forty-two states, the District of Columbia, and the federal government), only twenty-one executions had been carried out during 1963, half that of the next lowest year since 1930. As compared to 1930, when executions were carried on in thirty-two jurisdictions, in 1963 executions were carried out in only thirteen jurisdictions. Of forty-eight prisoners who had been sentenced to death, fifteen had their sentences commuted to life, one was transferred to a mental hospital, and the death sentences of the remaining thirty-two were reversed or vacated by the courts.

During the same period, 1930 to 1963, when the number of executions had declined from a high of 199 in 1935 to a low of 21 in 1963, the homicide rate had decreased from a high of over 9 per 100,000 population in 1930 to a low of less than 5 per 100,000 in 1963 (U.S., Department of Justice, *National Prisoner Statistics* [Washington, D.C.: Government Printing Office, 1964], pp. 4, 9).

volved, and that the release and employment of prisoners would represent only "an insignificant fraction of the total free labor force, either nationally or locally."[17] These assurances reflect the deterrents to progress in this field, which have persisted since Wisconsin led the way in 1913 with the Huber Law.[18]

Similar clashes of viewpoint and resulting compromises are to be found at the state level. Efforts to modify laws in the light of evidence from the social sciences or in the light of new knowledge about mental health are repeatedly opposed by those who threaten that change will lead to increased crime. Kalven and Zeisel have observed that "our new knowledge of human motivation has seeped into the law and deepened its concern with the causes of crime and the possibility of its cures. And the more we become aware of both the more precarious our traditional notions of guilt become."[19]

The states are still struggling with the question of criminal responsibility—under what circumstances a mentally ill person shall be freed from such responsibility, what his condition must be, and how far a psychiatrist shall be allowed to give all his findings and his opinion.[20] The M'Naghten Rule still remains a powerful deterrent to change, constantly invoked by those who are fearful of the "potential criminal" and who remain convinced that only the most rigid rules of responsibility will deter others from crime.

Even in legislation that acknowledges the problem of mental health as a significant factor in determining deviant behavior, one finds proposals to enlarge services accompanied by procedures to restrict the freedom of the individual for whom the services

[17] "The Prisoner Rehabilitation Act of 1965," *Federal Probation*, XXIX, No. 4 (December, 1965), pp. 3–7.

[18] *Ibid.* Although Senator Long wrote that one of the most obvious advantages of the authority created by the Prisoner Rehabilitation Act of 1965 would be "the expanded use of community resources in the treatment of psychiatric and medical cases," the Act did not provide for expenditures for such services.

[19] "Law, Science and Humanism," p. 342.

[20] In writing on the question of criminal responsibility, Sheldon Glueck states: "we must be content with a reasonably flexible standard, but one made as understandable and practical as the misalliance between law and psychiatry will permit" (*Law and Psychiatry*, p. 98). Instead of speaking of the relationship as a misalliance, I would prefer that we view it as a marriage fraught with both dangers and limitless potential for mutual enrichment.

are intended. This approach cannot be dismissed as caused solely by the lack of logic or understanding of lawmakers. It must rather be seen as an accurate barometer of the climate of prevailing attitudes toward mental illness and deviant behavior. Only last year a "master plan" for the care of the mentally ill and mentally retarded in New York State reflected these different attitudes and approaches. While recommending a liberalization of the M'Naghten Rule to provide greater latitude for psychiatric testimony, it also recommended involuntary commitment of alcoholics to state hospitals for the mentally ill even if they are legally sane.[21]

The strong response to social problems such as the use of narcotics may be well-intentioned, but its benefits may be short-lived and its long-term repercussions detrimental. Once the response has been institutionalized through law, its consequences also become institutionalized through the sanctions imposed. Since the enactment by Congress in 1914 of the law designed to reach the unauthorized suppliers of narcotic drugs, the drug user has had to depend on illicit sources for his supplies. His possession and use of drugs have in themselves become criminal offenses.[22] These restrictions have not been balanced by procedures adequate to help those who wish to be cured, and the services available for the addict have been inadequate and ineffective.

The federal government has recently supported major changes in the federal narcotics law which would allow an addict accused of federal crimes to choose medical care in a hospital instead of imprisonment. Where such a choice is made, the charge is to be held in abeyance if the defendant agrees to submit to an examination to determine whether (1) he is an addict and (2)

[21] In 1965 in New York, as in other states, the mental hygiene law was amended to include a new article dealing with alcoholism *Laws of New York*, c. 813). In the Declaration of Purpose, the first sentence read: "Alcoholism is recognized as a public health problem and an illness afflicting large numbers of persons. . . ." The Declaration continued: "The purpose of this article is to provide, within appropriations made available therefor for research into the causes and means of prevention of alcoholism, the utilization of modern methods for the care and rehabilitation and treatment of alcoholics and the evaluation thereof. . . ." Provisions were included for voluntary admission of alcoholics and for admission on the certificate of two physicians, accompanied by application of the nearest relative (secs. 306, 307).

[22] 38 Stat. 786 (1914), 26 U.S.C. Part 2554 (c) (1) 1946.

he is capable of rehabilitation. With these questions answered affirmatively, if the defendant chooses treatment he is to be committed to a federal hospital for no more than three years.

The questionable value of the punitive approach toward narcotics addicts is underlined by the definition of addiction by the World Health Organization, which covers both the physical and the psychological compulsion to use drugs.[23] The compulsive element in the craving of the drug addict was recognized by the Supreme Court in its holding that criminal punishment for being an addict constitutes cruel and unusual punishment.[24] Such appreciation of realities has not, however, been followed by any substantial modification of the punitive approach to the problem in most states or to the development of substantial treatment services, except in a few areas. While some states have provided for civil commitment of addicts, so satisfying those troubled by the penal language of the narcotics laws, the real question of what treatment is available after commitment still remains unanswered.

As in the treatment of the mentally ill, fear of the narcotics addict and demand for protection on the part of the general population invites disregard of both the rights and the needs of the addict. Even when a program for treatment is proposed, government officials feel forced to explain that the plan is directed toward controlling crime as well as providing treatment.[25] The use, non-use, and abuse of law to meet the problems of the narcotics addict reflect inadequate knowledge on the part of physicians, the readiness of legislators to "help" the addict while protecting the community against him, and the general unwillingness of society to pay the necessary price for adequate treatment. As a result, laws which subvert the rights of the addict, offer panaceas, and fail to provide essentials for treatment proliferate.

[23] United Nations, World Health Organization, *Technical Report Series 1950*, 21:6.1–6.4.

[24] *Robinson v. California,* 370 U.S. 660 (1962).

[25] See the report on the narcotics program by Governor Rockefeller, in *Albany Bulletin on Health & Welfare Legislation of the State Charities Aid Association,* January 4, 1967, p. 3: "The Governor expressed concern over citizens' lack of personal security from personal danger. . . . Addiction to narcotics is a major cause of crime; it is responsible for half the crime in New York City."

Confinement has been described in terms of treatment. The comment of the prosecutor that "the only difference between jail [sentence] and commitment is that in the hospital the beds are softer" may not be ignored.[26]

While the majority viewpoint among such august bodies as the American Medical Association and the National Research Council favors the extended use of voluntary hospital commitment of addicts, there is great difference of opinion as to the medical basis for determining who is an addict. There is not only the question of when a user becomes an addict but of whether the drug used shall determine how the user or addict is to be treated. In the legislative halls where the new statutes have been enacted, there is also confusion as to how long a person committed civilly shall be detained, who should be admitted to the treatment programs, and who shall determine an addict's release on the basis either of "cure" or of being found "incurable."

If addiction can be defined as "compulsive need," and if it is true that the physical craving can be removed quickly although the personal problems making an individual prone to addiction and recidivism may be deeply embedded, one must ask to what degree the methods of treatment provided under existing laws are geared to the addict's rehabilitation during his confinement. One must also ask to what degree the mechanism for dependency or escape in the addict is likely to be touched by treatment in prisons or any other forms of confinement provided by the state. How much can the judge be expected to know when review is sought? How much shall the judge rely on the director of a hospital, who may or may not know enough, who may want to keep or get rid of a patient, who may be quite remote from the individual patient and unable to give a satisfactory prognosis in the light of his history, problems, and potential?[27]

The sad fact remains that neither present legislation nor administrative policies have proven either effective or attractive to the addict. Individualized treatment, procedures for rehabilita-

[26] See *New York Post*, March 6, 1966, p. 27.
[27] See Ed Coller, "Civil Commitment of Narcotics Addicts," Paper prepared for the Welfare Law Seminar, New York University Law School, 1965.

tion, services necessary to maintain resistance to drugs, and plans to help the addict on his return to the community have been missing.[28] Compulsory commitment of addicts when no crime has occurred also raises serious constitutional questions as to whether society has the right to take away a man's freedom because of addiction.[29] The distinction made recently in England between crime and sin and the decision of the Parliament to regard voluntary homosexual relations between consenting adults as no longer a crime is relevant to our approach through law toward habits, mores, and attitudes that are repugnant to the majority of people. How far should law intervene to restrict the freedom of the individual? How far can we or should we seek to force a different way of life on the individual?

It is important that proposed legislation be scrutinized to determine whether it is geared to provide shortcuts rather than significant service for those caught in a way of life from which they wish to find an exit. Would outpatient clinics, medical care along with prescribed dosages of the addicting drug, personal service, and help in securing employment be a more effective method than the extension of "hospital" commitment? How far should law be used to restrict, to confine? How far should it be used to provide real services? What may be the results of these different methods? Do we know?

The psychiatric examinations of 4,500 drug addicts convicted of felonious crimes between 1954 and 1960 are reported to have shown a far lower incidence of psychosis, psychoneurosis, and mental deficiency than among the group of all persons convicted of felonies. In contrast, the percentage of what the authors of the study define as psychopaths was three times as high in the addict

---

[28] See Nathan Straus, *Treatment before Cure* (New York: n.p., November, 1965), p. 8: "Only 28 of the 615 addicts committed in 1963 to a civil hospital under the civil commitment law completed hospitalization and after-care programs satisfactorily enough to have the criminal charges against them dismissed by October 1964."

[29] See the criticism by the American Civil Liberties Union of the Rockefeller proposal for compulsory commitment for drug addiction, *New York Times,* February 27, 1966, p. 1. See also *Robinson* v. *California*, 370 U.S. 660 (1962).

as in the non-addict group.[30] From these findings (largely dependent on definitions for the purpose of classification and on the diagnostic ability of the court psychiatrists) the authors re-emphasize an earlier opinion that "the management of the great mass of adult criminal offenders is, and should remain, in the hands of penologists, judicial and correctional authorities, parole boards, and probation bureaus."[31] They assert that "this conclusion will remain valid as long as no effective psychiatric method or regime for the treatment of psychopaths is devised." They further assert that the statistical study "demonstrates" that "the problems of the drug-addicted criminal belong primarily in the realm of sociology rather than psychology or psychiatry—a conclusion that accounts in their opinion for the consistent failure of corrective measures developed from psychiatric premises." They conclude: "It is fatuous to hope to 'reform' the non-addicted psychopath by psychiatric means; it is doubly fatuous to expect psychiatry to achieve any substantial result with the drug-addicted psychopathic criminal."

The only positive recommendations in these two studies are for stronger measures to curb the illicit drug traffic and opposition to permitting the psychopathic drug addict to "cop out" to a minor plea and so secure a minimum period of incarceration. No evidence is presented as to the effects of shorter or longer periods of incarceration. More important, nothing is said about the substance or lack of substance of the psychiatrically oriented program for the criminal drug addict, which the authors condemn as useless. One must wonder why these psychiatrists, whose work was largely in the diagnostic area, selected sociology as the social science that held the greatest promise for reform. One can only speculate as to whether its generic attributes provided a remote and comfortable depository for an impossible task, or whether wishful thinking led them to believe that sociology could solve drug addiction along with all other human problems.

[30] Emanuel Messinger, M.D., and Arthur Zitrin, M.D., "A Statistical Study of Criminal Drug Addicts," *Crime and Delinquency*, XI, No. 3 (July, 1965), 283–92. The drug addicts (usually addicted to heroin) constituted 27 per cent of the general group.

[31] Emanuel Messinger, M.D., and B. Apfelberg, M.D., "A Quarter Century of Court Psychiatry," *Crime and Delinquency*, VII, No. 4 (October, 1961), 343–62.

In striking contrast to these defeatist conclusions as to the use of treatment for drug addicts are the early reports of the program in Maryland jointly undertaken by the Maryland Department of Mental Hygeiene and the Department of Parole and Probation. It is described by Dr. Lee Wurmser, a research psychiatrist, as an attempt to treat drug addicts outside a prison or hospital, using the threat of imprisonment if the patient fails to cooperate. Addicts are paroled from state penal institutions and returned to their homes and jobs, subject to frequent laboratory tests to determine any relapse. Regular treatment is required at a psychiatric clinic which provides group therapy and individual counseling. In a period of fourteen months a 50 per cent rate of success is reported, as against the less than 10 per cent of Lexington, Kentucky, patients who are not "rehooked" within six months after discharge.

Recent examination of the ways in which we deal with the problem of narcotics addicts has shown the wide gap between knowledge and its implementation through law. It has also shown the ineffective role of organized medicine in the face of a mounting threat to more and more people and of the tragic results both to addicts and their victims. To the authors of *The Road to H.*, the individual addict is seen as a casualty in the adaptive struggle for a rewarding human existence, whose failure elicits not sympathy and aid but scorn, persecution, and ostracism: "We think it high time . . . to call a policy forcing the addict from degradation to degradation, and all in the name of concern with his welfare, just what it is—vicious, sanctimonious, and hypocritical, and this despite the good intentions and manifest integrity of its sponsors."[32]

The care of the mentally ill was long regarded as a local responsibility. As a result of the disclosure of the tragically inadequate and uneven quality of local services, responsibility was transferred to state governments. Additional decades passed before it was recognized that adequate care of the mentally ill could only be approached if legislation were enacted to provide federal

[32] Isidor Chein, Donald Gerard, Robert S. Lee, and Eva Rosenfeld, *The Road to H.* (New York: Basic Books, 1964), pp. 378–79.

assistance to the states.[33] Even in New York, with its resources of money and manpower, comprehensive community-based programs that included preventive, treatment, and rehabilitation services were not planned until federal assistance became available.

In 1948 the Group for the Advancement of Psychiatry reported its deep concern about state laws governing commitment of the mentally ill.[34] It noted that commitment in the early statutes was limited to the dangerously insane and that therefore these and subsequent statutes had continued to attach the stigma of criminality to the mentally ill in varying degrees. Procedures included commitment by a jury (twenty-one states) by judges and commissioners (six states), by standing commissions appointed by a court (six states), by a judge and two physicians (twenty-three states), by a judge and one physician (eight states), by certification by two physicians (six states) and by non-judicial authority with two physicians (three states).[35] In addition to describing the procedures as anachronistic, the report discussed the harm done when a mentally ill person is exposed as a public spectacle and subjected to procedures used by the criminal courts. The Group also pointed out that these procedures were still being followed, as seen in the widespread use of jails to house the mentally ill.

---

[33] Until 1896, when the State Care Act was passed in New York, localities were required to pay a weekly rate to the state for the care of mentally ill in state hospitals. In 1954, New York enacted the first Community Mental Health Services Act. It provided one dollar per capita of population to each participating unit of local government on a matching basis. In 1963 the dollar limitation was removed. The resulting thirty-six county mental health boards and the New York City Community Mental Health Board were described as providing "services to 95 per cent of the state's population." While these boards may cover such a percentage territorially, no one can claim that they provide adequate services to the population. These statutes are still described as home rule laws, which leave it to each local government to determine what it will do. Whether its expenditures are adequate or not, they are matched by the state. Further laws have been enacted since 1963, so that comprehensive programs may move forward as federal funds become available and personnel is recruited.

[34] *Commitment Procedures* (Report No. 4; New York: Group for the Advancement of Psychiatry, April, 1948).

[35] See Note, "Civil Commitment of the Mentally Ill: Theory and Procedures," *Harvard Law Review*, LXXIX, No. 6 (April, 1966), 1289: "The procedures for applying the statutory tests varied as much as the tests themselves."

A uniform commitment law was urged that would permit certification by two qualified physicians, would safeguard the patient's right to a court hearing on a petition for release, and would provide for both emergency and voluntary hospital admissions for the mentally ill. Finally, the report listed five fundamental rights of mentally ill persons committed to hospital care that should be protected by law: (1) the right to communication with persons outside the hospital; (2) the right to periodic physical and psychiatric examinations; (3) the right to discharge as soon as possible; (4) the right to protection of civil rights unless revoked by law; and (5) the right to the benefit of the best existing techniques of therapy.

Today approximately one out of every ten persons enters a mental hospital as a patient at some point during his or her life. The roles of law and medicine in protecting the rights and welfare of such persons have therefore become of increasing importance. The goals of protection of the civil rights and the right to freedom, fair admission or commitment procedures and procedures for review, and assurance of early and adequate treatment are still far from achievement. Growing interest in the constitutional rights of individuals has helped to stimulate a reexamination of commitment laws in many states. In New York, following years of study, a new law became effective on September 1, 1965.[36] Its focus is on making voluntary and informal admissions easier and on establishment of procedures and training of personnel to protect the rights of patients. It provides for regular review of the status of each patient by both hospital authorities and the courts.[37] This law represented a compromise between those who believed that there should be far more comprehensive protection of the mentally ill and physicians who were apprehensive about the effects on the patient of continuing review of his case by lawyers and about the additional burden that would be placed on already overworked medical personnel.

[36] The study was stimulated in 1959 by Dr. Paul H. Hoch, then Commissioner of Mental Health for the State of New York.

[37] *Laws of 1964*, c. 738. See also Hyman M. Fortsenzer, M.D., *New York's Direction in Mental Health Services* (New York: The Council of State Governments, Autumn, 1964).

A study which preceded the new law[38] raised many questions that still remain unanswered in most areas of the country, and presented certain basic principles on which law and treatment of the mentally ill should be based:

> Every person with serious mental illness needs some care and in many cases must go to a hospital, even if he does not want to.
>
> Mental hospitals are not prisons, but they do, by force on body and mind, deprive patients of some freedom.
>
> Rapid non-compulsory admission to mental hospitals is good for mental patients and helps in allowing effective treatment and early release.
>
> When a patient must be sent to the mental hospital against his will, he should not be treated like a criminal and be tried and convicted of being sick. Procedures for his admission are only stepping-stones to treatment.
>
> Any person hospitalized against his will is entitled to watchful protection of his rights because he is a citizen first and a mental patient second.[39]

Examination of practices in various parts of the state had disclosed that "the policies of the hospital and the habits of local doctors and judges seem to determine the choice of method (of admission) far more than do the needs of the particular patient." The "vaunted flexibility" is described as an accidental diversity.[40] That this holds true not only of admissions but also of care, treatment, discharge, after-care, and the protection of the civil rights of the patients poses a problem of vast dimensions and great urgency to both law and psychiatry.

The same study also recommended safeguards for the protection of the patient's rights at all stages of his hospitalization and found the "need during the entire stay in a mental hospital for objective and periodic examination of a patient's status and right to release . . . essential to continuing protection of his rights

---

[38] Committee of the Association of the Bar of the City of New York, in cooperation with the Cornell University Law School, *Mental Illness and Due Process* (Ithaca, N.Y.: Cornell University Press, 1962).

[39] *Ibid.,* p. 14.

[40] *Ibid.,* p. 51.

as a citizen."[41] The importance of such safeguards is evident if patients are not to be lost or forgotten in state hospitals, especially if they are old, poor, and a burden to their families. A section of the Mental Hygiene Law, authorizing a hospital, upon certification of a single physician, to receive and retain any person suitable for care and treatment who does not object to such hospitalization had been attacked earlier by a New York court as one which "effectively shunts seniles into involuntary confinement without awareness of their plight and without their actual approval or judicial surveillance."[42]

The place to which a mentally ill person is to be committed may be determined by criminal law procedures, accidents of geography, or who is to pay for the care. The determination may be both inconsistent and utterly irrelevant to the needs of the patient. Thus in New York, the answers to such questions as whether the charge is an offense or non-indictable crime, whether an indictment has been returned or an information has been filed, and whether the cost of care will be chargeable to the state or the county may determine whether the mentally ill person is sent to a civil hospital or a hospital for the criminally insane. As the New York study concludes: "Such differing results are hard to justify, in the absence of any showing that they are based on the needs of society."[43]

Beyond this criticism there is also the question of the basis on which a person presumed to be innocent, until proven guilty, can rightfully be committed to the prison system for an indefinite period. Yet our laws authorize such action not only when a defendant is found to be suffering from such a severe mental illness as to be unable to stand trial but also when he is found not guilty by reason of insanity.

[41] *Ibid.*, pp. 19, 20–21. The study's recommendation for a new state-wide agency, independent of existing departments and responsible to the courts having jurisdiction over admissions and discharges, was enacted into law in 1964. The Mental Health Information Service created under the law was given responsibility for advising patients of their rights and preparing the facts on which the court could base an informed judgment.

[42] See Justice Brenner in *Matter of Jones*, 9 Misc. 2d 1084, 1085, 172 N.Y.S. 2d 869, 870 (Sup. C. Kings County 1958).

[43] Committee of the Association of the Bar of the City of New York, *Mental Illness and Due Process*, pp. 220–39.

The dangers inherent in concentration on legal procedures without examination of the results of their use was dramatized by the disclosure of the conditions at the Bridgewater, Massachusetts, State Hospital, administered by the Department of Correction with "supervisory" powers resting in the Department of Mental Hygiene. It was reported that 2,000 alcoholics, sex offenders, defective delinquents, and persons suffering from general mental disorders were housed there in 1,200 cells without flush toilets; 75 "patients" were living in a former locker room 50 by 100 feet in size. Described by a judge in testimony before a special legislative committee as belonging somewhere in the seventeenth or eighteenth century, regarded as "hopeless" by professional staff in the area, it was the catch-all for many persons whose problems cried out for treatment but whom old laws, unwieldy administrative procedures, and outright indifference to their rights and to their welfare had buried there.[44]

The terrible fear that a person acquitted of a crime because of insanity will be released to work further havoc has undoubtedly played a part in the apathy of the public toward the conditions that have continued in institutions for the "criminally insane." Somehow, it has not been realized that release or condemnation of the criminal to such conditions are not the only alternatives. A defendant acquitted of a crime because of insanity may by law be automatically committed to a civil hospital by the court that heard his case. A federal statute authorizing such action has been upheld as constitutional.[45] The same fear has caused states to keep in institutions for the criminally insane after their sentences have expired defendants who were convicted, were later found insane, and were placed in those institutions. In 1966 the United States Supreme Court unanimously held that such retention of a convicted person after his sentence expired violated his rights, and that he was entitled to treatment in a civil hospital.[46] The petitioner in the Supreme Court ruling had

[44] "Reform Is Urged in Mental Health," *New York Times*, January 29, 1967, p. 43.
[45] *Ragsdale* v. *Overholser*, 108 U.S. App. D.C. 308, 281 F.2d 943 (1960). Cf. *Lynch* v. *Overholser*, 369 U.S. 705 (1962).
[46] *Baxtrom* v. *Herold*, 383 U.S. 188 (1966).

been certified as insane by a prison physician shortly before the expiration of a two-and-one-half-year sentence for second-degree assault. He had been transferred to a state hospital under the jurisdiction of the state Department of Correction. At the expiration of his original sentence the director of the state hospital at the prison filed a petition for civil commitment. The court signed a certificate that the respondent "may require mental care and treatment" on the basis of medical certificates from two examining physicians and that he was still mentally ill and in need of hospital and institutional care. The respondent was not represented by counsel and stated he had no objection to being transferred to a civil hospital. However, the Department of Mental Hygiene had determined *ex parte* that the respondent was not suitable for care in a civil hospital. He was, therefore, retained at the prison hospital after the expiration of his sentence until released by the decision of the Supreme Court.

The Supreme Court unanimously held that "petitioner was denied equal protection of the laws by the statutory procedure under which a person may be civilly committed at the expiration of his penal sentence without the jury review available to all other persons civilly committed in New York." The Court also held that the petitioner was further denied equal protection of the law by his civil commitment to an institution maintained by the Department of Correction beyond the expiration of his prison term without a judicial determination that he was dangerously mentally ill.

The importance of review by the United States Supreme Court in individual cases where the rights of a single individual are involved is illustrated by this case. A writ of *habeas corpus* by the prisoner had been dismissed. This dismissal was affirmed by the intermediate state court, and motion for leave to appeal had been denied by the New York Court of Appeals. As a result of the decision by the Supreme Court, six hundred inmates in the hospitals of the state prison system were "quietly" transferred to civil hospitals under the jurisdiction of the Department of Mental Hygiene. At the time of this transfer the officials of both the Correction and Mental Hygiene Departments were described as concerned about what they called the "panic" and "crisis of confidence" that could result from misunderstanding of the transfer by the public. The *New York Times* quoted one mental hygiene official as saying, "You can imagine what would happen if the public should get the idea we are turning raving maniacs loose on society."[47] In the same article it was reported that the State Attorney General's office was watching to see whether they would be deluged with claims for money damages for illegal confinement. The New York State Court of Claims had just awarded $115,000 to a man who had been held in the Dannemora Prison Hospital for twenty-four years after the expiration of his sentence; he had been convicted of stealing five dollars' worth of candy.

Additional questions not reached by the Baxtrom case remain. These include whether there is any basis in law for commitment to the prison system, or to a hospital under the system's jurisdiction, of a person who has not been convicted of a crime, but is found to be "dangerously mentally ill." The question as to what extent this practice is derived from traditional concepts that fused the mentally ill with the criminal, and kept such patients under lock and key as a substitute for treatment demands answers in terms of what treatment such people are entitled to receive and of their constitutional rights. A further and more basic question, also unanswered by the Baxtrom case, remains as to whether action taken under statutes authorizing commitment of the mentally ill for hospital care can be upheld where custodial security rather than appropriate medical care and treatment is all that is provided.[48]

While the New York study stressed the importance of medical admissions and procedures for voluntary and informal admissions so as to encourage early treatment with a minimum of trauma or stigma, it did not examine the quality or diversity of quality of treatment in state hospitals. That such a study under

---

[47] "State Is Shifting Mental Inmates," *New York Times*, March 19, 1966, pp. 1, 23.

[48] At the Senate hearings in 1961 it was reported that one half of the patients in state hospitals receive no treatment at all and that in most public mental hospitals the average ward patient comes into person-to-person contact with a physician for about fifteen minutes each month ("Civil Commitment of the Mentally Ill," p. 1289).

impartial medical auspices is needed to raise the level of treatment in state hospitals is clear. The disparity between numbers of discharges and numbers of commitments in just two receiving hospitals in New York City underlines the difference in standards.[49] In addition to studies on the state level, it may well be necessary that the federal government, which has begun to finance mental health programs, undertake studies in depth and establish standards of care as a condition for federal aid.

Certainly federal financial aid has brought some hope to a generally bleak outlook in that it has acted as a spur to state and local governments to create community mental health centers associated with local hospitals. There is growing support for the position that the mentally disabled should be given treatment in hospitals close to their homes and no longer put away and isolated in vast institutions that provide only custodial care. It has been shown that when treatment is made available, as in the state hospital in Kansas, under the influence and with the aid of Menninger, hospitalization can be drastically shortened, with financial as well as human savings.

The hospitalization of the mentally ill again demonstrates the need for changes in the law and the limitations of laws if they are not made meaningful through services to the people for whose benefit they are enacted. There is need to guard against concentration on procedural reforms, no matter how well intentioned, either as a substitute for providing services or as an end in themselves.

Concern about sex offenders has led to a spate of sexual psychopathy laws, of which California's, passed in 1939, was one of the earliest.[50] By 1949 the law required that, after a plea of guilty

---

[49] Committee of the Association of Bar of the City of New York, *Mental Illness and Due Process*. In 1960 Bellevue Hospital admitted 17,477 patients to its psychiatric division and discharged 52 per cent of them. That same year Kings County Hospital admitted 10,871 patients and discharged 34 per cent. The average length of stay for observation was almost identical.

[50] Illinois, in 1938, was the first state to enact such a statute (see *Illinois Revised Statutes*, c. 38, secs. 820.1–825 [1957]). The Minnesota act was upheld as constitutional by the U.S. Supreme Court in 1940 (see *Minnesota* ex rel. *Pearson* v. *Probate Court of Ramsey County*, 205 Minn. 545, 555, 287 N.W. 297, 302 [1939], aff'd 309 U.S. 270 [1940]).

or conviction for a sex crime involving a child under the age of fourteen, the defendant be committed for ninety days for a clinical determination as to (1) whether he was predisposed to committing sex offenses, and (2) whether he was a menace to the health and safety of others. If he was considered amenable to treatment, he was then recommitted to a state hospital for an indeterminate period. Subsequently, if and when the superintendent of the hospital was of the opinion he was no longer a menace, he was to be returned to the original committing court for sentence or probation.

A study of recidivism among the sex offenders so treated (including a sample of 1,921 males) and committed as "probable sexual psychopaths" reported that the cumulative recidivism rate during the five years studied was 26.6 per cent.[51] This report pointed up the error of citing a categorical recidivism rate for sex offenders, since the rate varied from 18.2 per cent for pedophiles with female victims to 40.7 per cent for exhibitionists and 46.8 per cent for the combined category of voyeurs, transvestites, and lewd persons.[52] While acknowledging that psychiatry offers no magic cures, and that controversy as to the most effective treatment for personality and character disorders involving sexually deviant behavior continues, the author asserts that experience has shown that custody alone "solves neither the social nor the personal problems of the sex offender." Three-fourths of the 1,921 sexual psychopaths treated had not reverted to sexually deviant behavior, as measured by absence of a new sex offense conviction over a five-year period. They were reported to have achieved healthy interpersonal relations and positions of social and occupational respect, in direct challenge to both law and psychiatry.

In its report, *The Mentally Disabled and the Law*, the American Bar Foundation states that with the exception of Michigan and California the sexual psychopath statutes have not been widely used.[53] The sexual psychopath laws and the penal laws

[51] Louise Viets Finsbrie, "Treated Sex Offenders Who Reverted to Sexually Deviant Behavior," *Federal Probation*, XXIX, No. 2 (June, 1965), pp. 52–57.
[52] *Ibid.*, p. 55.
[53] P. 303.

against other sexual offenses, often enacted under the impact of some widely publicized sex crime, have been subject to criticism on many counts. The assumptions on which laws against sex offenders have been based have been questioned by the Group for the Advancement of Psychiatry. After a three-year study the Group reported that the preponderance of persons who carry out sex offenses for which they are punishable under current law are not involved in behavior fundamentally different from that commonplace in the population; such persons are not necessarily to be regarded as suffering from psychiatric disorders or as socially dangerous.[54] Thus the popular demand for indefinite incarceration based on the notion that such offenders are abnormal fiends, dangerous, and insane is quietly negated. Unfortunately, such studies have not lessened public clamor for their incarceration or its effects on legislators and trial judges. There is general acceptance of the assumption that the sex deviate is more dangerous than other criminals.[55] The assumption that sexual psychopaths have higher recidivism rates than other offenders has also been shown to be incorrect by a series of studies.[56] Another assumption—that sex offenders or deviates progress from minor to major sex crimes—has also been challenged by studies of the evidence.[57] The assumption that there can be a clear definition of the class of persons to whom sexual psychopath statutes are applicable has been proved false by the American Bar Foundation study. Twenty-eight different definitions or descriptions of the personality of the sex deviate were found in the statutes of the twenty-seven states that purport to deal with this same personality in their laws.[58] Finally, as some studies have shown, the mere passage of legislation authorizing hospitalization of sexual

[54] *Psychiatrically Deviated Sex Offenders* (Report No. 9; New York: Group for the Advancement of Psychiatry, May, 1949, rev. February, 1950).

[55] The report of the Illinois Commission on Sex Offenders (1953) stated that "not more than about 5% of convicted sex offenders are dangerous" (*The Mentally Disabled and the Law*, p. 304).

[56] See P. Tappan, "Sentences for Sex Criminals," *Journal of Criminal Law and Criminology*, XLII, No. 3 (September–October, 1951), 332–37: "Our sex offenders are among the least recidivous of all types of criminals. They do not characteristically repeat as do our burglars, arsonists and thugs" (p. 336).

[57] *The Mentally Disabled and the Law*, p. 304.

[58] *Ibid.*, p. 305.

psychopaths, even if they could be defined, does not create hospital space, treatment facilities, or personnel, and the "treatment" has been found to be almost purely custodial. In one state a separate cell block was set aside in the state prison for sexual psychopaths.[59] The American Bar Foundation report concludes that "lack of treatment destroys any otherwise valid reason for differential consideration of the sexual psychopath."[60]

The danger of the assumption that laws authorizing treatment will lead to treatment is illustrated by what has happened under the New York sex offender law providing for indeterminate sentence. Dr. Abrahamsen, who had studied sex offenders at Sing Sing as a member of a commission, supported this law. He described it as "designed to provide for the rehabilitation, treatment, and release of sex offenders who suffered from some form of mental or emotional abnormality and at the same time to provide for the continued care of those who clearly were still a danger to society."[61] The law was approved unanimously by the legislature in March, 1950. The New York Commission's proposal for an institute where such defendants could be treated and research carried forward was scrapped. By 1955 even the research project on sex offenders at Sing Sing was given up: "the implementation of the law has come to a standstill," Dr. Abrahamsen wrote in 1960.[62] In the absence of treatment and review of cases the judges quite properly became reluctant to sentence offenders to prison for periods ranging from one day to life.[63]

Law, with its criminal sanctions, has been the institution invoked to control and punish not only sexual psychopaths but

[59] *Ibid.*, p. 307. The Illinois Commission on Sex Offenders reported that one institution had four hundred patients and only one part-time psychiatrist.
[60] *Ibid.*, p. 308.
[61] David Abrahamsen, M.D., *The Psychology of Crime* (New York: Columbia University Press, 1960), p. 177.
[62] *Ibid.*, p. 178. In 1953 Minnesota enacted a sex offender law which provided for mental examination and made psychiatric treatment mandatory for convicted sex offenders judged able to benefit by it. In 1960, Dr. Abrahamsen reports, not one person had thus far been recommended for treatment; he also notes that no funds had been made available for the purpose (pp. 265–66).
[63] See *People* v. *Kaganovitch*, 23 App. Div. 2d, 4th Dept. 183 (N.Y. 1965): "Adequate psychological and psychiatric services are indispensable to the whole concept of 'one day to life' sentences and without them the 'one day' is meaningless and the 'life' may well be the end result."

those who violate the approved mores in regard to sexual conduct. The question of how the criminal law should formulate its provisions relating to sex crimes and crimes against the family was on the agenda in 1964 at the International Congress on Criminal Law, attended by six hundred delegates from fifty countries. As Rapporteur General to the conference, Judge Ploscowe noted that "people's views as to the harmfulness of specific sexual behavior are influenced in large measure by their religious training, cultural background, and ethical predilections. As a result views vary from individual to individual, and from country to country." He expressed the view that "law enforcement is never very effective in dealing with behavior that occurs secretly and is consented to."

In his report of the decision of the delegates[64] he makes the following points: (1) there was no support among the delegates for provisions found in many state penal codes punishing a single act of fornication; (2) the consensus of opinion was that adultery should no longer be made subject to criminal sanctions, and should be solely a matter of family law; (3) penal law revisions were recommended to make possible adequate sociological and psychological studies of those who engaged in an act, so that penal treatment would be based on such findings; (4) the criminal law should not prohibit the dissemination of birth control information or the distribution of contraceptives except to juveniles; (5) a compromise resolution on abortion was approved provided that the penal law, while prohibiting abortion in principle, should make it permissible where: (a) it is necessary to preserve life, physical or mental health, or stability of the mother; or (b) where the pregnancy is the result of rape or incest or where there is a probability that the child will be deformed; (6) a resolution was adopted against making the act of artificial insemination a penal offense, but it was recognized that criminal sanctions may be invoked when the consent of the husband is not obtained; (7) homosexual and deviant sexual activity should continue to be a punishable offense where: (a) force or violence

[64] Morris Ploscowe, "Report to The Hague: Suggested Revisions of Penal Law Relating to Sex Crimes and Crimes against the Family," *Cornell Law Quarterly*, L, No. 3 (Spring, 1965), 425–45.

is used; (b) a minor is involved; (c) an adult abuses a position of trust; (d) public scandal results from open behavior; or (e) there is homosexual prostitution.

It is significant that the decisions of this assembly, representing countries regarded as far less libertarian than the United States, should in each area have recognized the wisdom of reducing criminal sanctions against individuals in seven areas in which our own penal codes remain largely unchanged. In the comment on homosexual behavior, it was noted that present penal laws affecting such behavior when conducted in private had become largely a dead letter, beneficial only to the blackmailer.[65]

This position is strongly supported by a recent study, *Sex Offenders*.[66] In his review of this work Dr. Robert Coles notes that

> among other interesting points made by the studies one finds that, "contrary to popular notion, sexual crimes are by no means likely to be associated with force, violence, drug addiction or even exposure to the stimulation of pornographic literature. In large measure those who molest children are sad, lonely, bewildered people who try to fondle rather than in any sense rape them, and usually bungle the effort, attract attention, and invite the arrest they may unwittingly want. . . . Very few states really try to find out which offender is actually dangerous."[67]

Dr. Coles deplores American rhetoric on crime, the warnings on the loosening of morals, the dangers of the cities, and the threat of alien philosophies. He finds the sex offender paraded as the example of all corruptions of which we must rid ourselves. He is dismayed that getting tough with such people is equated with

---

[65] The now famous Wolfenden Committee in England published its recommendation that homosexual practices in private between consenting adults should no longer be treated as criminal. It was in this report that the Committee sought to establish a distinction between crime and sin. For criticism of this report, see Lord Devlin, *The Enforcement of Morals* (Oxford: Oxford University Press, 1965); Ronald Dworkin, "Lord Devlin and the Enforcement of Morals," *Yale Law Journal*, LXXV, No. 6 (May, 1966), 986–1005.

[66] Paul Gebhard, John Gagnon, Wardell Pomeroy, and Cornelia Christenson, *Sex Offenders* (New York: Harper and Row, 1965).

[67] Robert Coles, "Anatomy of Perversion," review of *Sex Offenders*, in the *New Republic*, October 16, 1965.

patriotism and normality while programs for rehabilitation are begrudged adequate funds.

With the growth of legislation to meet personal, social, and business problems has come a proliferation of administrative agencies. Regulatory agencies have been created to determine fair prices for gas, power, and telephone service, to safeguard the right of labor to organize, to prevent conspiracies in restraint of trade, to supervise radio and television station operations, to prevent deceptive advertising, etc. In every such area there is implicit an expansion of the role of law in the life of the community and of countless individuals. Like other agencies and arms of government the commissions, set up to make swift and sound decisions, have been deluged by the massive scope of their responsibilities and by new technological developments to cope with which they have neither training nor sufficient personnel.[68]

The administrative agencies created to implement social legislation face overwhelming problems. Welfare agencies, health agencies, public hospitals, child care institutions, and correctional institutions are confronted by a population explosion triggered not only by population growth but by legislatively mandated services. The funds, the personnel, and the necessary training and development of new procedures lag far behind the mandates imposed by law on these agencies. The illusion that laws create services or can be self-fulfilling continues to linger, to the detriment of those for whose benefit they are enacted. Concentration on laws rather than the development of a process through which law can be made meaningful in the lives of people has been commented on by an English lawyer who has observed the struggle for racial equality in the United States: "The commitment of the Federal Government and thousands of Americans to the

---

[68] Newton N. Minow has described the problems of a regulatory body such as the Federal Communications Commission—the F.C.C.'s inability to keep up with its tasks and the way in which technology has changed what was regarded as the significant role of selecting among would-be television licensees to something that is quite meaningless (*The Mazes of Modern Government: The State, the Legislature, the Bureaucracy, the Courts* [Santa Barbara, Calif.: Center for the Study of Democratic Institutions, 1964]).

struggle for racial equality is impressive but . . . it appeared that sufficient political energies had not yet been directed to improving the *process* by which law is administered, rather than the laws themselves."[69]

Administrative agencies and the courts have by action and inaction helped to condone and perpetuate the illusion that laws, as presently administered, are fulfilling the purposes of legislation. The vast number of individuals whose lives are directly affected by the administrative machinery established to implement legislation imposes the requirement that administrative agencies be constantly re-examined to see how close they come to fulfilling the legislative mandate imposed on them. The obligation to report honestly what can and cannot be done with the personnel and funds available is essential if myths of service are not to take the place of honest confrontation with realities. The population now subject under law to administrative decisions is so large that constant scrutiny to determine how the process is affecting individuals is necessary. Self-policing is a rare art, and improved methods must be developed for securing the facts from those who are directly providing or withholding services and from those who receive or are denied such services. Here the process of judicial review becomes significant. While the courts, like administrative agencies, have at times engaged in perpetuating myths, they have the opportunity in test cases to scrutinize the facts and reject the fraudulent pretense of service, establish standards, and provide guidelines. The courts have the power to impose the constitutional safeguards essential to the protection of individual rights.

In recent years, as noted earlier, appellate courts have shown increasing concern with what happens to the rights of individuals under the administration of law by police, administrative agencies, and the courts. In a recent decision the U.S. Supreme Court pointed out that the courts as an independent branch of government are apt to be more "responsive . . . to the constitution-

---

[69] Anthony Lester, *Justice in the American South* (London: Amnesty International, 1964).

ally protected interests" than are administrative agencies created to do a special job, and that therefore prompt access to the courts is a constitutional requisite.[70] However, what the vast extension of the rule of law, through legislation and its administrative agents, will mean to countless human beings, to their self-respect, to their hopes, and to the protection of their rights will depend largely on the concern for their rights and welfare by those who shape and work within the new institutional structures.

There is no field where the illusion that laws create services or can solve individual problems prevails more widely than when they are enacted to protect society from the mentally ill or the socially deviant. The United States Court of Appeals for the Fourth Circuit recently reversed the conviction of a chronic alcoholic with direction to release the defendant unless, within ten days, the state should be advised to take him into civil remedial custody.[71] In another recent case, the United States Court of Appeals for the District of Columbia held that proof of chronic alcoholism was a defense against the charge of public intoxication. The court held it was error for the trial judge to refuse expert medical and psychiatric testimony that the defendant was an alcoholic who had lost control over his consumption of alcoholic beverages.[72]

In commenting on this decision, the *New York Times* noted that the court had referred to a law passed in 1947 requiring commitment for medical treatment rather than correction and imprisonment in cases of drunkenness. It commented that the 1947 law was written so as not to go into effect until adequate treatment facilities were provided, and that because this had never been done the law had never been applied. In fact, although there were forty thousand arrests made each year for public drunkenness, the District still had only thirty-five beds set

---

[70] See *Freedman* v. *Maryland*, 380 U.S. 51 (1965).

[71] *Driver* v. *Hinnant*, 356 F.2d 761 (4th Cir. 1966). The defendant had spent twenty-five of the preceding thirty-six years in jail as a result of some two hundred similar convictions.

[72] See "Ruling Barring Jail for Chronic Drunks Ignored," *New York Times*, April 10, 1966, p. 56; *Easter* v. *District of Columbia*, 361 F.2d 50 (D.C. Cir. 1966).

aside for alcoholics in the general hospital, and these were reserved for patients suffering from serious side effects or from other diseases.[73]

Welfare departments have had to face more and more problems created by family disorganization due to mental illness, severe emotional disturbance, mental deficiency, and interpersonal inadequacies. As negative pressure to get families off welfare has grown, along with positive pressure to rehabilitate individuals and families, the skills and the resources for such work have been found to be lacking. Critical decisions as to whether individuals should be hospitalized or children removed from their families are made, ways of dealing with the problems of the unmotivated, the alcoholic, the narcotics addict, the ambulatory schizophrenic, and the unemployable are set up—all by investigators without professional training. The psychiatrist available for diagnostic examination in the case seen as urgent or dramatic is unavailable in the vast majority of cases.

In the Family Court of New York one repeatedly sees the tragic results of administrative failures, of denials of benefits provided by law, lack of adequate funds, and untrained personnel with titles and power incommensurate with their interests or abilities. Too heavy case loads and insufficient supervision also play a part in negating the substantive and procedural rights of human beings.

Thus in a petition filed by a "case worker" on behalf of the New York City Department of Welfare, the mother of seven children was charged with neglect. The "social worker" testified that he had visited the home in November, 1965, when the mother and six children were living in a four-room apartment which he found disorderly and foul-smelling. The mother was pregnant. A further statutory visit was made three months later. The mother had now delivered the seventh child and was back in

[73] *New York Times*, April 1, 1966, p. 31. In his article, "Arrests for Public Intoxication" (*New York Law Journal*, May 3. 1967, p. 1), Judge Murtagh speaks of "arrests for public drunkenness as a status offense. . . . the offense consists in being a derelict. The immediate condition of inebriety may be the occasion, but it is not the fundamental reason for an arrest."

the apartment with the four-day-old infant. No homemaking service had been provided. No effort to rehouse the family had been made. A neighbor had cared for the six children while the mother went to the hospital but had returned to her own home at the time of this visit. The one phrase reiterated by the petitioner for the Welfare Department was that the mother had been "non-cooperative." The record of the Department of Welfare on this case went back to 1959. There was a history of the home being dirty and cluttered and of repeated misuse of welfare funds. No assistance in housekeeping had ever been given the mother. Four days after her last baby was born, at the time of the social worker's visit, no recommendation had been made for assistance although she had the responsibility for the new infant and six other small children.

When the "case worker" was asked what action had been taken to improve the situation, he spoke of the restriction of rent on various occasions as the "assistance" rendered by the department. He further stated that he had not noticed that the children were unusually small in size and unable to talk. He did not know that they had been suffering from malnutrition until after the mother had been arrested. No medical reports on the family had been obtained. Even though two of the children were known to be retarded, they had not been referred for a psychological examination. When questioned as to why no recommendations had been made regarding these children, the court was told that it was not the function of the welfare worker to make recommendations in regard to children.

When the children were found alone in the apartment by the police, they were taken to a shelter. The shelter worker testified that they were in very poor condition, dirty and hungry. The three older ones were unable to communicate and the two younger ones had to be sent at once for hospital treatment of severe malnutrition. The medical social worker at the hospital testified that the two children (aged seventeen months and three weeks, respectively) were in a condition of extreme emaciation when admitted. This was twelve days after the case worker had visited the home and noticed "nothing" about the children.

At the hearing that followed the mother testified:

When I was carrying my last baby, I asked Mr. C.—my light and gas was restricted—I told Mr. C. because I mailed the light bill to him and it was cold—it was cold and I could just hardly stay home with my kids. I brought them back and forth to H's house to stay. When I come back out of the hospital, it was the same over again. He again tried to do nothing. I begged him and sometimes he made me mad.

In the long run the merit of social legislation will be determined by two factors: the development of services essential to translating legislative purpose into reality and the provision of adequate safeguards to protect the rights of the individual subject to the legislative program. In turn, these will depend largely on the training and concern of those who work within the new institutional structures and on the courts who review their operations.

Administrative practices set up under legislation directed to protect and support the weak must not be permitted to make men weaker and more dependent. Constant vigilance will be required if the meaning of freedom is not to be lost in the "benevolent" maze through which an increasing number of individuals must find a path in order to survive.

Chapter III

CHASMS BETWEEN NEW CONCEPTS
AND PRESENT PRACTICES

The mythical figure of Sisyphus is remembered for the fruitless task assigned him. He was made to roll a big boulder up a mountainside, only to have it roll down again, thus forcing him to repeat the task endlessly. In some ways the approach of law and medicine to the troubling and troubled people in our society differs from that of Sisyphus only in that so many of their representatives seem satisfied with the task assigned. Laws to punish the criminal, the alcoholic, the narcotics addict, and the sex offender are enacted; prosecutors present their cases; stiff sentences are mechanically handed out, especially when the press is agitated.

Attorney General Katzenbach was recently quoted as saying before a congressional committee that "Far too many lower courts now operate on an assembly line basis. . . . We must give priority to finding ways to end the disgraceful meat grinder character of these courts."[1] Offenders and sick people are arrested, confined, and temporarily removed from the community and from sight, only to be released to return to old haunts and to the behavior that originally produced the symptoms of their problems —which remain untouched, unmodified, and persistent. They are again apprehended, and all the machinery of law is once

---

[1] *National Council on Crime and Delinquency (NCCD) News*, XLIV, No. 4 (September–October, 1965), 2. A colleague of mine whose assignment had been changed from the Family Court to the Criminal Court said he was no longer so tired in the evening. His explanation was that he had to move so fast that he could not even try to make contact with the individual defendant, much less think about what should or could be done for him.

more solemnly invoked to demand another "payment to society," which in its turn once more foots the bill.[2]

Throughout the process, so long as the role of medicine and psychiatry remains minor, it is certainly equally fruitless. Diagnostics are ordered by the court before trial to determine whether the offender can distinguish between right and wrong; diagnostics are ordered before sentencing to help determine where the defendant is to be incarcerated; diagnostics are again used to determine whether the defendant is accessible to treatment or how he should be categorized. These studies, with some exceptions, rarely lead to opportunities for a man to discover himself, his potential strengths, or the way to a more healthy or constructive use of his life.

Modifications in laws and procedures to handle deviant behavior or mental illness suggest that more emphasis is frequently placed on technical administrative improvements than on substantive changes in services needed to help those for whom, theoretically, the system is administered.[3] We have also constantly modified or "improved" the legislation governing our children's courts by increasing their jurisdiction beyond the delinquent to include the neglected child, family support, family offenses, separation, and divorce. However, we have not enlarged their authority to secure the services needed to handle these problems.

In 1958, almost fifty years after the initiation of the first juvenile court psychiatric clinic, Dr. Manfred Guttmacher reported that there were only eleven juvenile courts in the whole of the United States that had child guidance clinics as an integral part of their organization. None of these had been established during the preceding decade. The voices and efforts of both law and psychiatry had not been heard. Little had been done to edu-

[2] Sheldon Glueck reports that on the basis of intensive follow-up studies over the years it has been "demonstrated beyond reasonable doubt that the product of routine penal administration is much more likely to be recidivism than reform" (*Law and Psychiatry*, p. 136). See also Harold F. Vehling, "Crime Breeds on Smothered Feelings," *Federal Probation*, XXX, No. 1 (March, 1966), 11–16.

[3] Despite statutory provision for state hospitalization of alcoholics in thirty-six states and for drug addicts in thirty-four states, such admissions account for only 4 per cent and 1 per cent, respectively, of all first admissions (see *The Mentally Disabled and the Law*, pp. 18–19).

cate judges, and, in a period of expanding psychiatric teaching, psychiatric case seminars for the probation staff were non-existent except in a few places such as Baltimore.[4]

Too often the courts have been used to put away people with problems rather than to help them master their problems. On the basis of my many years' experience as a judge, I must question why decisions as to medical treatment of juvenile offenders are left in the hands of the judge: is it that the community is more concerned with its own protection than with the healing of the deviant child?

It seems as though too many members of the mental health profession have accepted without question the role of auxiliary aids, props to be used or rejected in matters which fall primarily in the area of their own knowledge and which are appropriately their responsibility.

The civil servant-psychiatrist, who is all too frequently separated from the vital growth of knowledge in his field, sometimes becomes more moralistic in his judgments than scientific in his evaluations. Even the language such physicians use betrays the growing separation between them and their profession. Like many of the children sent to them for study, these physicians have lost their sense of identity. No longer part of the mainstream of psychiatric thought, they seem to draw strength from the law's power to pass judgment and from a moralistic application of value judgments.

This strange transformation of roles was evident in the case of an intelligent eleven-year-old truant, caught in the crossfire of rejection by a father who had abandoned his family to live with another woman and by a mother who had turned to promiscuous relations following nightly excursions to neighborhood bars. The psychiatrist described the family problems as the cause of the boy's disturbance and reported that the child presented no psychotic trends and that he repressed his anxiety and hostility behind a responsive and happy façade. However, he then added: "It would seem that he is selfish with his planning in that he compels his parents to focus attention on him by his deviations."

[4] *The Mind of the Murderer*, pp. 135–36, 142–43.

The dominant community concern with self-protection is reflected in the image of the judge as an authoritative figure who has the power to decree punishment and exile from the community. It is reflected in the custodial character of institutions used for the offender, be he child or adult. It is also reflected in the allocation of tax funds, a most tangible expression of what a community is prepared to do.[5] Finally, it is reflected in the public's periodic demand that the juvenile court stop coddling delinquents and return to the "good old-fashioned" forms of punishment.[6]

Throughout the vast majority of our courts and institutions overcrowding and understaffing prevail. Without the benefit of basic facilities or services for adequate care of children and adults, we have introduced the clinician. His efforts to individualize, to secure the child's or adult's history, to seek understanding of the psychodynamics of the patient, and to explore alternative methods of treatment may sometimes appear like the proverbial geranium used to adorn the window of a house of ill repute.

The judge, the parole officer, the probation officer, the prison guard, and the institutional counselor continue to face stark realities in making dispositions and providing custodial care. The absence of responsibility for disposition or care on the part of the clinician becomes an understandable source of irritation, noncommunication, and even distrust. When the clinician also evidences indifference toward what must or can be done by those charged with administering the law or providing care, he is resented as more concerned with his professional status than with the problems that he confronts.

The vague popular assumption that mental health programs have made a substantial contribution in the correctional field is

[5] See *Local and State Expenditures for the Administration of Criminal Justice in New York State* (Albany, N.Y.: State of New York, June, 1965). Of $502 million spent in 1961–1962, 70 per cent went to police services, 2 per cent to probation, and 1 per cent to parole services for forty thousand persons. Auxiliary services, including expenses for medical examiners, coroners, and psychiatrists, were allocated 1 per cent. Institutions administered by the state received 20 per cent of this sum.

[6] Justine Wise Polier, *Back to What Woodshed?* (Public Affairs Pamphlet No. 232; New York: Public Affairs Press, 1956).

extravagant. While concepts and attitudes derived from mental health teaching have surely affected what many people in all ranks of correctional service say and even do, the widespread absence of meaningful mental health programs negates the assumption. Two experienced clinicians in Wisconsin write: "It is sometimes difficult to determine whether psychiatric personnel are seen as useful partners or are merely tolerated as necessary status symbols."[7] Pacht and Halleck examine the reasons why, after a half century of thought and writing on the need for a psychodynamic approach to the understanding and treatment of criminals, this situation should exist. With candor they point to the record. Most mental health workers, particularly psychiatrists and psychologists, have avoided meaningful involvement in correction. Their pleas, usually uttered from a safe distance, have little effect. They oversell the virtues of the psychodynamic approach. There is a vast discrepancy between what the literature says that the clinician can do and what the relatively inferior clinical personnel in correctional institutions actually do or can do. There is far too little understanding by clinical personnel of the problems and realistic anxieties of those charged with the care and control of criminals in our prisons or of the limited role of such personnel in a prison setting. The authors also point out that the prisons in this country are still, for the most part, custodial fortresses, with punishment a major ingredient in the prison regimen. Where the dignity and worth of the individual are ignored, the milieu is at odds with a therapeutic approach.

Given all these problems, it is perhaps not surprising to find that the *Manual of Correction Standards* in 1960 states: "The precise achievements and ultimate potential of counseling, casework, and clinical services are as yet largely unknown. . . . It is largely 'an educated opinion' which underlies the demands for increased professional services. In time there must be a concrete demonstration of the 'pay off.' "[8] In Massachusetts one of the most significant mental health programs in the correctional field

[7] Asher R. Pacht and Seymour L. Halleck, "Development of Mental Health Programs in Correction," *Crime and Delinquency*, XII, No. 1 (January, 1966), 1–8.

[8] American Correctional Association, *Manual of Correction Standards* (New York: By the Association, 1960), p. 16.

has been developed. This program includes aid to probation, parole and judges, staff training, diagnostic services, treatment services, and research. Yet, its architect, Dr. Leon N. Shapiro, acknowledges that only a small percentage of the prison population has been reached, and expresses the hope that the prison system may "be slowly changing its judgmental view into a more curious one."[9]

In our juvenile courts, as in our correctional institutions, with rare exceptions, both the quality of mental health personnel and the heavy burdens placed upon them have contributed to restricting the value of their services. In the courts, as in the correctional institutions, they have been given neither a manageable nor a challenging role. The exclusive task of providing diagnostics for a steady stream of children and parents to be processed on the basis of single interviews unrelated to further disposition, treatment, or research can hardly be expected to invite the interest of first-rate professionals. Where, in addition, the clinic in the juvenile court is segregated from the probation services, it becomes even more insular and therefore frustrating to a physician concerned with the mental health of the individual patient and what can be done for him.

It is significant that in both Wisconsin and Massachusetts, where valuable models of service have been slowly developed, the local universities and training hospitals have been brought into the picture. These programs have thus received valuable yeast from young physicians in training, who can and are expected to learn through service to courts and institutions. The additional teaching and research opportunities have helped to attract and hold in these programs people of the caliber essential for raising the level of service.

There are also certain negative factors that members of the mental health professions have increasingly recognized as of their own making. For too long in too many courts, correctional institutions, children's institutions, and social agencies a professional hierarchy has been established. At the apex stands the psychiatrist, often in isolated and self-isolating splendor. Below

---

[9] "Psychiatry in the Correctional Process," *Crime and Delinquency*, XII, No. 1 (January, 1966), 16.

him ranks the psychologist, then the psychiatric social worker, and below him the "generic" social worker. Still further down one finds the probation officer and the child-care worker, the people who live with or work with the people whom this hierarchy is intended to serve. Finally, at the bottom, one finds the custodians and the maintenance people.

More and more members of the mental health profession are discovering that in work for and with people, team work must involve everyone and remove such status stratifications. Roles may be defined without denigrating the significance of service. Only recently, an able psychiatrist working with emotionally disturbed children presented a case which illustrates this comparatively new awakening. He described a very difficult psychiatric session in which a child was confronted with the fact that a man he believed to be his father was not, in fact, his father. Several hours later the child, feeling shattered and lost, caused an upheaval in the residence. It was the child-care worker whom he attacked. It was to her he said, "You can't like me. I'm nobody. I don't know who I am." It was she who told him that he was the same boy to her he had always been, who comforted him, and who gave him the solace at night essential to sleep—and to awaking ready for the morrow.

In the field of correction and rehabilitation of human beings whose behavior is deviant, limited psychiatric services are being weakened and fragmented by two contradictory forces. We find increasing demands on mental health workers to provide the treatment that will make the individual whole, productive, and a functioning member of society. At the same time society demands that mental health experts shall diagnose and prognosticate, if not prophesy, which individuals engaged in deviant behavior should be walled off or sealed up indefinitely so as to protect the community.

Prisons and state mental hospitals have been held responsible for what has been described as "the unnecessary crippling of the mentally ill." They must be re-examined not only in terms of their functioning but in terms of their utilization by the larger society. Dr. Robert C. Hunt, Superintendent of the Hudson River State Hospital, has pointed out that much of the regressive behavior of the mentally ill is artificially created, a by-product of the conditions under which they are detained. He notes "the virtual disappearance of antisocial and irresponsible behavior when patients are treated and trusted as responsible fellow human beings." He expresses great impatience with those who would make the state hospitals the whipping boys of American psychiatry and suggests that larger budgets and increased staff might do much to correct the basic flaws in our system. He places the responsibility where it belongs when he writes: "Our society *hopes* for successful treatment, but it *demands* safe custody of those whom it rejects."[10] Hunt describes the pressure for security embodied in the architecture, laws, rules, and customs of these institutions, and the acute irritation of the public when something goes wrong. At such times it takes courage for any hospital superintendent not to tighten security, in the face of excoriation by the judiciary, crucifixion by the press, and other forms of harassment.

Every word written by Dr. Hunt is equally true of the conditions in our prisons, our correctional institutions, and even in many detention homes and institutions for children. Every word is also true of a society that hopes for rehabilitation of the offending adult and child, but continues to demand safe custody for those whom it basically rejects. After some dramatic and publicized offense by a child, I have heard colleagues speak of their increased use of detention. Hospitals which are courageous enough to release children on parole, when they believe it is indicated from a medical point of view, are criticized vehemently when a child again acts out, as though all children should be retained until they were absolutely "safe."

There is an irrational demand for security against the known offender or person who has been found to be mentally ill that is utterly inconsistent with the individualization of treatment or the concept of rehabilitation. It sometimes seems as though we feel justified in ridding ourselves of any threat from such people

---

[10] "An Approach to the Prevention of Disability from Chronic Psychoses, Part I," Address to 34th Annual Conference of the Milbank Memorial Fund, 1957; quoted in Joint Commission on Mental Illness and Health, *Action for Mental Health* (New York: Basic Books, 1961), pp. 47–48.

once they have been identified and given numbers. Certainty is demanded in areas where certainty is not yet possible, and fear restricts thoughtful and meaningful progress in treatment and rehabilitation. In the words of the Joint Commission on Mental Illness and Health:

> People do seem to feel sorry for them [the mentally ill] but in the balance, *they do not feel as sorry as they do relieved to have out of the way persons whose behavior disturbs and offends them.*
> . . .
>
> As a reaction to deviant behavior, rejection is, of course, a well-established characteristic of any social group. Society depends on a system of order, conformity, solidarity; it uses rejection as a threat to exact thorough individual compliance with the expectations of the group.[11]

These words are applicable to the offender whether adult or juvenile.

The stigma of mental illness or of anti-social behavior continues to pursue both the patient and the defendant, whether adult or child. The person released from a mental hospital or correctional institution is not regarded as an ordinary convalescent by family, friends, neighbors, or prospective employers, including local, state, and federal governmental bodies.[12] Despite all assurances to the contrary, this attitude also applies to the juvenile delinquent, whose record is used to bar him from civil service jobs, the air force, officer training programs, and private employment. The broad chasm between new concepts and actual practices is again illustrated by the general lack of after-care and of halfway houses to help rehabilitate both the mentally ill and those who have been in correctional institutions. Such facilities are almost non-existent. In 1958 there were only nine halfway houses and only eight rehabilitation centers in the United States for the mentally ill. Dr. Jack Ewalt, Director of the Joint Com-

---

[11] *Action for Mental Health*, p. 58. It is pointed out here that about one in one hundred persons in the United States becomes mentally ill to a degree that results in diagnosis and hospitalization. Yet "lacking in effective moral strength and medical means to help this one person in 100, society has organized itself out of primary concern for the 99 who behave in tolerable fashion . . ." (p. 87).

[12] *Ibid.*, p. 60.

mission, notes the periodic attempts to provide more humane care for the mentally ill but adds that "while each reform appeared to have gained sufficient ground to give its supporters some sense of progress, each has been rather quickly followed by backsliding, loss of professional momentum, and public indifference."[13]

The improvement in the care of the mentally ill is largely limited to the physical care of patients, and little progress has been made in transforming state hospitals from custodial to therapeutic institutions. The lot of the 80 per cent of those hospitalized psychiatric patients who are inmates of state hospitals is to receive the lowest daily expenditure per patient and the lowest ratio of employees to patients.[14] This figure of 80 per cent represented 839,644 human beings in 1957.[15] With the rapidly increasing number of patients who enter mental hospitals, the role of law as well as medical care in psychiatric patients' lives take on new dimensions. Despite tinkering with state laws, which largely affects admission and discharge procedures, the drastic changes needed to assure early and adequate treatment and the protection of the "rights" of the patient are far from being secured.[16]

What is called "treatment" in state hospitals for the mentally ill is highly variable. The proud statistics of shorter hospital stays despite an increase in admissions and readmissions may reflect good treatment and earlier return to the community under outpatient care. However, they may reflect only overcrowded conditions and the pretense of aftercare pending another crisis, or they may reflect the use of drug therapy to remove what have

[13] *Ibid.*, p. xxix.

[14] *Ibid.*, p. 18. Veterans Administration psychiatric hospital cost per patient day is three times as high and the cost per patient day in voluntary psychiatric hospitals is four times as high as that of the state hospitals.

[15] *Ibid.*, pp. 22–23. The Commission expressed the belief that over one half of the patients in most state hospitals receive no treatment of any kind designed to improve their mental condition.

[16] *Ibid.*, pp. 107–10. The World Health Organization reported that in 1949 only 10 per cent of admissions to state hospitals in the United States were voluntary, as compared with 70 per cent in England and Wales. The study ascribes this situation to the restriction of civil rights and the overcrowded conditions of state hospitals (see also *Mental Illness and Due Process*).

been called the "more florid symptoms of mental illness while leaving the disturbance itself untouched."[17]

In reports and descriptions of various institutions one notes the vast differences in range of services. One finds wishful thinking that so often conceals the absence of service. One finds rare structures that include skilled staff in numbers that can make work meaningful and programs that provide continuity of service to inmates and their families.[18] One also finds an institution in which treatment of sixteen hundred criminally insane persons and sex offenders is approvingly described in an article as based primarily on teaching inmates to minister to one another. The professional teaching staff for this population numbers two. The rest of the educational effort, like most of the therapy, is left to the patients! The whole program sounds like a sociologist's dream and a physician's nightmare. Ward councils, executive councils, general assemblies, self-help, and control by fellow patients seems to present a picture of democracy gone mad. The real answer to the question, "What about individual treatment methods?" is finally given: "The limited number of qualified therapists available does not permit extensive use of individual therapy."[19]

A second explanation given in the article for the development of what is described as a multiple group program, but what is in reality a self-help program run by the criminally insane, is the "ominous silence" in the professional literature about "the effectiveness of individual treatment for patients who are from the lower socioeconomic group and have strong anti-social tendencies or severe character disorders." What is not explored is why patients from the lower socioeconomic groups have never

[17] Dr. Mortimer Ostow, Chairman of the American Psychoanalytical Association Study Group on Drugs, quoted in the *New York Times*, December 5, 1965, p. 69.

[18] See Harold M. Boslow, M.D., and Sigmund H. Mannes, "Mental Health in Action: Treating Adult Offenders at Patuxent Institution (Maryland)," *Crime and Delinquency*, XII, No. 1 (January, 1966), 22–28.

[19] Arthur E. Elliott, "A Group Treatment for Mentally Ill Offenders (Description of Atascadero State Hospital, a Maximum Security Institution in California)," *Crime and Delinquency*, XII, No. 1 (January, 1966), 29. Mr. Elliott was Chief Social Worker and Training Officer at Atascadero State Hospital from 1963 to 1965.

received their share of good individual treatment from physicians, clinics, or social agencies, any more than they have received a fair or even minimal share of other worldly goods. In the place of treatment the complacent assertion is made that there is no evidence that individual treatment is effective. There seems to be a lack of awareness of the extent to which lack of healthy interpersonal relationships have dulled or destroyed hope and therefore motivation for healthy functioning. The anomie that has dogged these people's lives is then rationalized as a justification for non-treatment. A sociologist concludes that "unrealistic optimism (on the part of largely untrained staff expected to help these sick people) has become tempered in the day-to-day contact with patients whose pathology blunts any type of therapeutic intervention." The use of new sociological instruments for the purpose of experimentation has taken over in the absence of all treatment. The guinea pigs are the thousands of criminally insane hidden away behind locked doors, for whom no one speaks.

In Elliott's description of Atascadero State Hospital one finds all five of the stigmata of "maladjustive dehumanization" described by Dr. Viola W. Bernard and her colleagues: (1) increased emotional distance from other human beings; (2) diminished sense of personal responsibility for the consequence of one's actions; (3) increasing involvement with procedural problems to the detriment of human needs; (4) inability to oppose dominant group attitudes or pressure, leading to self-directed dehumanization to secure relief; and (5) feelings of personal helplessness.[20]

The National Commission on Mental Health noted that the question of exactly what percentage of patients diagnosed as psychotic could with treatment be returned to the community and lead useful, satisfying lives is constantly raised. In striking contrast, no such questions are raised concerning research, humane treatment, or surgical intervention when the disease under review is physical. Surgeons do not hesitate to report prognoses of a 5

[20] Viola W. Bernard, Perry Ottenberg, and Fritz Redl, *Dehumanization: A Composite Psychological Defense in relation to Modern War* (Palo Alto, Calif.: Science and Behavior Books, 1965); reprinted from *Behavioral Science and Human Survival.*

to 15 per cent rate of cure for persons with cancers of the lung and stomach; on the contrary, they record the statistics, publish percentages of "five-year-cures," and find professional satisfaction in each percentage point of gain.[21] It is clear that a double standard is applied in the demand for promised or proven "cures" in regard to the child or adult who becomes mentally ill or involved in juvenile delinquency, criminal conduct, the use of narcotics, or alcoholism.

The failure to establish control experiments in efforts to improve the administration of justice has been explained on the grounds that to provide one kind of treatment for part of a group and to withhold it from others might violate "the law, with its supreme notion of equality, which cannot easily tolerate such discrimination."[22] Despite lack of precedent for controlled experiments and resistance to the notion of using human beings as "guinea pigs," Professor Zeisel argues that scientific experimentation is worth careful consideration if we are to "advance our notion of law as a rational means of social control." The hard fact is that "experimentation" and "inequality" are being practiced extensively without the benefit of observation and evaluation of results.

As an example, two children involved in identical delinquent acts, both of whose diagnostic reports indicate the need for residential treatment, may be subject to utterly different dispositions by the same juvenile court. On the basis of age, sex, race, religion, or simply bed space, one child may be sent to a residential treatment center, the other to a custodial institution with no treatment services. In similar fashion sentences to correctional institutions or hospitals result in entirely different treatment, depending

[21] A follow-up study was done of one hundred patients with acute psychosis committed to Boston Psychopathic Hospital in 1946 who were given intensive, individualized treatment. At the end of five years, seventy-six were living in the community, twelve were in mental hospitals, four had left the state, and eight were dead. The study notes that, while "in the community" did not mean cure, the use of social recovery as the yardstick of success in psychiatric treatment requires no apology. "Recovery" has the same general meaning when used in relation to many physically disabling diseases, including heart diseases, cancer, arthritis, and asthma (*Action for Mental Health*, pp. 24, 34–35).

[22] Hans Zeisel, "The New York Expert Testimony Project: Some Reflections on Legal Experiments," *Stanford Law Review*, VIII, No. 4 (July, 1956), 730.

upon the institution. The indifference or ignorance of judges, the inability or unwillingness "to fight the system," and inadequate facilities may explain but not justify such discriminatory treatment. The lack of follow-up studies to determine the results of such treatment only insulates those directly involved and the community from a sense of responsibility. If we honestly faced what is happening, lawyers, judges, and the community might be far more willing to permit scientific and control experiments directed to improving current practices, instead of granting or denying services to individual defendants without disclosure of the basis for such decisions.

Arguments, presented without substantiating evidence, as to the comparative benefits of custodial care versus treatment, harsh punishment versus "coddling," and retraining versus imposing obedience provide no guidance. Mental health experts, after a study of the needs of children for psychiatric services and the provision of such services in New York, acknowledged that "for decades, solutions to the problems have promised a new era in dealing with some of the major social problems of our society— the inadequate adult, the juvenile delinquent, the criminal and the sociopath." The report then frankly states that "the disparity between this promise and the service available to fulfill it often seems a cruel hoax to those called upon to deal with the psychiatric problems of the children."[23] In the first national report on patients of mental health clinics, it was found that of every ten patients for whom clinic services were terminated, eight had received a diagnostic evaluation but only three of the eight had received treatment. The other two had received a partial evaluation, had been referred elsewhere for a diagnosis, or had been given some "other services." For most patients services were terminated after a few interviews.[24]

[23] Report of the New York State Mental Health Planning Committee Task Force on Children, March 26, 1965 (manuscript), p. 1.
[24] See *Action for Mental Health*, p. 51, citing Anita K. Bahn and Vivian B. Norman. See also Sylvan S. Furman, Lili G. Sweat, and Guido M. Crocetti, "Social Class Factors in the Flow of Children to Outpatient Psychiatric Faculties," Paper Presented at the American Public Health Association annual meeting, November 14, 1963. In this paper the authors report that the public

In the final report of the Joint Commission the last paragraph in the summary of recommendations states:

> The outstanding characteristics of mental illness as a public health problem are its staggering size, the present limitations in our methods of treatment, and the peculiar nature of mental illness that differentiates its victims from those with other diseases or disabilities. It would follow *that any national program against mental illness adopted by Congress and the States must be scaled to the size of the problem, imaginative in the course it pursues, and energetic in overcoming both psychological and economic resistances to progress in this direction.*[25]

In the introduction to the report, Dr. Ewalt speaks of "the curious blindness of the public as a whole and psychiatry itself to what in reality would be required to fulfill our well publicized demand that millions of the mentally ill have sufficient help in overcoming the disturbances that tend to immobilize their self-respect and social usefulness."[26] He speaks of the embarrassment that would result if one placed reality and our pretensions side by side.

The avoidance of responsibility for difficult cases is fostered by the lack of adequate psychiatric services and the impossible pressures that are imposed on physicians attached to courts. It sometimes seems as though the mentally ill child is made a shuttlecock bounced back and forth through the courts by physicians as they attempt to score points against each other. Thus a fifteen-year-old boy, held in detention for stabbing a teacher, was transferred to a hospital because of his bizarre communication and behavior. A severe head injury with unconsciousness four years earlier had been followed by fear of crowds, the feeling that people were talking about him, and both visual and auditory hallucinations involving a blond Egyptian lady. He felt urges to kill at times, and had once attempted to kill himself

---

agencies serve 75 per cent of the patients and that their case loads outnumber those of voluntary agencies by three to one. The public agencies provide treatment to only 5 per cent of their case loads. In comparison, the voluntary agencies provide treatment for 40 per cent of the children in their case loads.

[25] *Ibid.*, p. xxiii.
[26] *Ibid.*, p. xxvi.

with a knife. The diagnosis was of schizophrenic reaction, paranoid type, and the boy was committed by one court to a state hospital. Within three months the state hospital requested his removal. Without reference to or evaluation of the consequences of the head injury, the boy was described as constricted, isolated, and seclusive. The hospital officials reported to the juvenile court: "he is considered potentially dangerous, and although this is increased by his impulsivity and poor controls, he is considered responsible." The hospital stated that the boy was unlikely to be helped by hospitalization, gave the diagnosis of "primary behavior disorder, conduct disturbance," and paroled him on aftercare pending court action.

During his later remand to the detention home by the juvenile court, the psychiatrist who had originally referred him for observation found primary and secondary signs of schizophrenia. Though less tense than eight months earlier, he expressed discomfort with people and spoke of his feeling that people were looking at him and talking about him. The boy was seen as "not only potentially but manifestly dangerous." The psychiatrist raised the question of what one should do with a dangerous youngster repeatedly diagnosed as suffering from schizophrenia, and asked whether it was fair to him or to the other boys to place him at the state training school. He added that "while such practice frequently occurs it is by no means logical either medically or sociologically." In the light of his rejection by the state hospital, the court was forced to place the boy at the training school.

There are many sources of confusion which impede progress in the application of what we know. These include not only conflicting opinions of experts but more basic conflicts in attitudes toward sex, delinquency, crime, mental illness, and all types of deviant behavior. Practical problems also arise, such as how many people can be contained, imprisoned, and treated, and how much it will cost. Finally, our society has become so dehumanized that it is not moved by the miseries and wrongs done to people whom it does not see, and at the same time humanized to the degree that it is disturbed from time to time by the disclosures of the legal perpetration of cruel punishment or of the withholding of treatment from the mentally ill. We are unwilling to pay for great programs of change and yet are made uncomfortable by our sins of omission. We want to get rid of the threatening individual and also be assured that getting rid of him is in his best interest. As we begin to look more closely at what we do and fail to do, we find ourselves ill prepared for great plans or for the initiation of programs to meet newly recognized necessities. We weave and waver. The result is an irrational deployment of existing services away from those who are in greatest need and distraction of attention from the preventive measures that will be most effective.

In the area of child care the use of services to prevent maladjustment, to aid children in their own home, and to provide early diagnostic and treatment services is still unusual. When the child is removed from his own home, a diagnosis may be provided. It is only when the child is found too disturbed or mentally ill for care at home or in an ordinary child care setting that we invest in "expensive" mental health services. In similar fashion all types of adult offenders, including burglars, narcotics addicts, alcoholics, and sex offenders, are placed in prison, where individualized treatment is rarely available. Usually no treatment is provided until the offender becomes obviously psychotic, and then it may remain little more than token.

Chapter IV

INDIVIDUALIZED JUSTICE IN OUR SOCIAL COURTS

Social courts in this country originated in the juvenile court movement at the beginning of the century. The juvenile courts were entrusted with applying two revolutionary concepts in the development of law. The first was that a child was a growing and changing human being who should not be treated by the law as an adult. The second was that the purpose of the law in dealing with a child was to rehabilitate rather than punish him. It was envisioned that such courts would concern themselves with the specific problems of each child and then seek such services and treatment as were best suited to his needs. This positive concept was and still is described as "individualized justice."

The law has accepted this concept to the extent that juvenile and family courts have now been established by the legislatures of every state. In 1964 it was reported that there were 2,800 courts that hear juvenile cases. In that year these courts heard 686,000 delinquency cases and 150,000 cases involving neglect or dependency.[1] It is tragic that the pioneering zeal which inspired the creation of these courts and the community support which secured the legislation was dissipated as the courts became accepted institutions. The implementation of the legislative directives has proven impossible because the means to fulfill the responsibilities imposed by law have, for the most part, been withheld by the legislative and executive branches of government.

[1] U.S., Department of Health, Education, and Welfare, *Juvenile Court Statistics, 1964* (Children's Bureau Statistical Series No. 83; Washington, D.C.: Government Printing Office, 1965).

The juvenile and family courts, while being given greater juris-diction over various types of family problems with a view toward achieving a less fragmented approach, have been handicapped by niggardly support, inadequate personnel, and a lack of proper facilities. In addition, while these courts have been hailed on special occasions as essential to strengthening family life, they have been treated as low man on the judicial totem pole, not only defined as "inferior courts" by statute but generally treated as less important than the courts which deal with property or adult criminals.[2] The bar has tended to regard such courts with kindly but aloof condescension.

As recognized in a recent volume, *Standards for the Juvenile and Family Courts*,[3] "individualized justice is not easy to achieve." This volume lists three elements essential to its achieve-ment: (1) a judge and staff identified with and capable of carry-ing out a non-punitive and individualized service; (2) sufficient facilities so that dispositions may be based on the best available knowledge and each child shall receive the care and treatment best adapted to his needs and to the protection of the community; and (3) procedures to assure that each child shall be considered individually and that the legal and constitutional rights of each child and his parents shall be duly considered and protected. The authors frankly acknowledge that "few if any courts have been able to meet all of these criteria" and that since their inception the juvenile courts have often found themselves without com-munity resources with which to make effective their judgments on behalf of children.

A recent study of judges in the juvenile courts[4] revealed that nearly one fourth were not lawyers licensed to practice and that

[2] U.S., Department of Health, Education, and Welfare, Children's Bureau, in Cooperation with the National Council on Crime and Delinquency and the National Council of Juvenile Court Judges, *Standards for Juvenile and Family Courts* (Children's Bureau Publication No. 437; Washington, D.C.: Govern-ment Printing Office, 1966), p. 28: "Over 50 per cent can be classified as inferior courts or branches of inferior courts of limited jurisdiction. The latter group might be categorized as having short judicial tenure requiring few if any qualifications for appointment of the judges and very low salaries."

[3] *Ibid.*

[4] Shirley D. McCune and Daniel L. Skoler, "Juvenile Court Judges in the United States, Part I: A National Profile," *Crime and Delinquency*, XI, No. 2 (April, 1962), 121–31.

they lacked the "basic professional credentials deemed essential to preside over any court." In answer to a questionnaire, 33 per cent of the full-time juvenile court judges who reported stated that they had no probation officers or social workers in their courts. For rural courts only, the figure was 54 per cent. Of the judges who reported 83 per cent stated that they did not have the help of any psychologists or psychiatrists. The study concluded:

> "the profile of the juvenile court judge and his work . . . offers an image of a part time judiciary, large components of which do not have adequate professional preparation or opportunity for in-service training and which operate under difficult caseloads and without adequate resources to properly discharge their assigned responsibilities. . . ."[5]

In Part II of this study, the working styles, characteristics, behavioral styles, work preferences, and values held by judges, probation officers, social workers, and police youth officers were measured through a series of tests and self-reports. The following findings were reported:

1. The judges more frequently report that, as adolescents, they were obedient and eager to please their parents or guardians rather than independent, rebellious and resentful. Their political, religious and social views are closer to those of their parents, and they are more inclined to believe that laws and social conventions are seldom or never useless and do not hamper individual freedom. They also much more frequently say that moral principles come from an outside power higher than man rather than that moral principles are relative and depend on circumstance.[6]

2. Judges and lawyers emphasized punishment, and social or welfare workers emphasized showing people the consequences of their actions.[7]

3. Other differences related to response to authority and degree to which they view moral principles as absolute or relative. Police youth officers were most likely to prefer routines and to believe that moral principle came from an outside power higher

---

[5] *Ibid.*, p. 131.
[6] Regis H. Walther and Shirley D. McCune, "Juvenile Court Judges in the United States," *Crime and Delinquency*, XI, No. 4 (October, 1965), 384–93.
[7] *Ibid.*, p. 388.

than man. Social workers are least likely to prefer routines and more likely to view moral principles as relative and dependent on circumstance. On each of their scales the judge occupies a position between the police officer and the social worker.[8]

In the light of these reports on the judges and the general absence of training for the work of the social courts, it is not surprising that the concept of individualized justice for each child has too often become justice peculiar to the attitude, knowledge, and values of the individual judge.[9]

A study of judicial action by successive judges in one large juvenile court[10] demonstrated that what happened to the children before the court largely depended on which judge was sitting. This conclusion was based on the number of adjourned cases, the extent of use of detention for delinquent children and parole for neglected children, the proportion of children placed on probation, and the readiness to explore plans other than commitment to a state school. Varying judicial attitudes more difficult to measure are also reflected in the way in which a judge speaks to a child or his parents at a moment in their lives when they are most vulnerable to humiliation or open to help—in short, how the power of individualized justice over others is used or misused.

The expectation that a lawyer, by donning the judicial robe, will be able to administer "individualized justice" when decisions depend in substantial part on an evaluation of the child and family that must be based on knowledge derived from medicine

---

[8] *Ibid.*, p. 390.

[9] U.S., Department of Health, Education, and Welfare, Children's Bureau, National Probation and Parole Association, and National Council of Juvenile Court Judges, *Standards for Specialized Courts Dealing with Children* (Washington, D.C.: Government Printing Office, 1954), p. 1:

The essential philosophy of the juvenile court has been called "individualized justice." This in essence means that the Court "recognizes the individuality of a child and adapts its orders accordingly," that it is a "legal tribunal where law and science, especially the science of medicine and those sciences which deal with human behavior, such as biology, sociology, and psychology work side by side," and that its purpose is remedial and to a degree preventive, rather than punitive.

[10] Justine Wise Polier, *A View from the Bench* (New York: National Council on Crime and Delinquency, 1964), pp. 1–3.

and the social sciences is absurd. No judge, however able or concerned, can hope to apply such knowledge at crucial moments of decision without preparation and guideposts from disciplines that are usually unknown to him when he ascends the bench. The expectation that he can do so reflects the assumption that, while expertise is necessary in all other aspects of the law, anyone and everyone can wisely determine what is best for other human beings.

It has only been in the last few years, through foundation support and federal aid, that some training programs have been undertaken for judges in the social courts. Whether independently or as a reaction to this new source of training funds, some law schools and medical schools have recently shown greater interest in the courts that are working with the problems of troubled people. In recent years, some juvenile court judges have turned to law schools and psychiatrists for sessions in which they could explore common problems. At some such sessions there has been an exploration of problems in a way that suggests new methods of dealing with people and provides helpful insights. At others, there has been a rather aggressive approach by some psychiatrists which might be described as an attempt at shock therapy. When the latter technique is used, it seems to be accompanied by abysmal ignorance on their part of the realities with which judges must deal. At one session in a large metropolitan area, where judges must still face calendars with over forty cases in a day and psychiatric diagnostics are done in half a dozen widely scattered clinics and hospitals, it was proposed that the judge should sit down with the psychiatrist in each case to focus and define the question he had in mind at the point of referral.

The pervasive lack of mental health services in the juvenile courts has not only impeded learning by judges but has frequently contributed to skepticism by judges and probation officers about the value of such services.[11] Even in those few priv-

---

[11] Dr. Henry Makover, a consultant to the New York Family Court, reported after a survey of a sample of cases that the diagnostic studies done by the court clinic seemed to have no real effect on what the judges decided at the dispositional hearing (see minutes of meeting with the Citizen's Committee for Children of New York, October 17, 1964).

ileged social courts where a psychiatrist is available for diagnostic purposes, he is seldom specially trained to work with children. The procession of troubled children and the time pressures that allow only a few moments for collateral interviews with parents and a family history from a probation officer (generally not professionally trained) limit the diagnostician to the surface symptoms. The value of a single interview with the child, who is often fearful of the unknown consequences of revelations about himself or his family, is at best limited.

With only diagnostic help of this sort, some judges, after observing the interaction between child and parents and hearing the testimony, may feel forced to pit their lay judgment against that of the psychiatrist. Others may be unduly awed and may even attribute some occult power to the psychiatrist which enables him to discover "the secrets of a stranger at a glance." If so, they automatically follow "the word," and fail to exercise their duty to make the final decision on all the evidence. There are, according to Anna Freud, exceptional analysts who have a flair for turning otherwise arid and unrewarding surface manifestations into meaningful material. However, such men are rarely to be found in the service of the courts. Even if they were, the limited role of the diagnostic study must be recognized:

> Even more discouraging for the efforts of the diagnostician are those symptoms which are identical in appearance but derived from mental sources which are in complete contrast to each other. Delinquent behavior in a child, for example, allows no immediate deduction as to the form of upbringing which has produced it. Without showing any difference in the overt result, it can be derived equally well from over-indulgence and lack of parental control as from excessive severity and emotional starvation.
>
> With the surface appearances as misleading as they are, symptomatology of this kind at the diagnostic stage is open merely to description. Without subsequent analytic investigation it offers few possibilities for assessing either the genetic or even the dynamic aspects of the case.[12]

[12] Anna Freud, "Diagnostic Skills and Their Growth in Psycho-Analysis," 1963 (manuscript).

Yet it is rarely that a court receives more than such descriptive help on which to base its decisions.[13]

The limitations of the diagnostic services in the social courts and even their absence are less devastating than the absence of the day-to-day services and resources which the courts need. The periodic attacks on the social courts for "coddling" young criminals and the allegations that the increase in delinquency proves that "treatment" does not work should be restated to acknowledge the fact that "treatment" has rarely been tried. In the limited number of cases in which a judge can secure skilled services for a child we can see what might be accomplished through "individualized justice"; they pose a challenge to those who are concerned with the welfare of children.[14]

In the case of one lad, nearly sixteen, who was brought before the Family Court of the State of New York for persistent truancy, investigation disclosed that he had been caring for a grandmother who was an alcoholic and a mother who was a narcotics addict. Having cared for these two women to the best of his ability—care which included searching for his mother and bringing her home when she became ill—he saw the court's intervention as treating him as an infant and interfering with what he regarded as his responsibility. Fortunately, he was assigned to a sensitive graduate student who was doing his field work in the court. The boy was able to speak to the student worker about his anger toward people who dismissed his mother and grandmother as worthless. He talked of the good things in his home that others could not see, including the family's love for each other. He told of how all his grandmother's children, except his mother, had

---

[13] It has been reported that, following a joint study by the state bar and medical associations of Massachusetts, mental health services were established for the courts of original jurisdiction. They included consultation, treatment services, training of personnel, and research. This program is regarded as all but unique among courts of original jurisdiction.

[14] In 1960 it was estimated that some 13,200 probation officers were needed to staff the juvenile courts. Of that number, only 4,400 were actually employed, and of these only 10 per cent had full graduate training (see U.S. Department of Health, Education, and Welfare, *Standards for Juvenile and Family Courts*, pp. 107–8).

become ashamed of her when they "made good" and abandoned her. Finally, he was able to express the fear that he too might do so. After weekly sessions with the graduate student, he was able to accept placement in a group therapy setting, on the condition that he would be free to visit home and not abandon his family. He was enabled to return to school and develop plans for his future while maintaining his loyalties. Unfortunately, this solution was largely the result of good luck—of the presence of a rare case worker who was drawn to and able to understand this boy. Without such help, in view of his age, poor school record, membership in a minority group, and discouraging home situation, commitment to a state school would have been seen as the only answer.

The social courts must stop functioning as lids to contain troubled people, as screens to conceal problems, or as institutions whose façades reveal little of their real capacity. With the growing concern for the social problems of our urban areas, the traditional well-intentioned social and civic agencies understandably try to enlarge the jurisdiction of the social courts. Legislators welcome social legislation from such sources that appears humane, and governors are not likely to veto it, especially if only a small price tag accompanies the benevolence.

For the social courts, the premises on which enlarged jurisdiction is urged are those of the treatment and rehabilitation of the juvenile delinquent, the care and treatment of the neglected child, or the strengthening of family life through case work and treatment services. The validity of these premises, however, depends not on buildings, clerks, or judges alone, but in large part on the services, both in their quantity and their quality, made available to the courts. It is at this point, just as much as in the planning for a public health service, that the help of the social scientists and mental health experts is essential. Yet, while they are occasionally invited to read a paper or make a speech at a later stage of planning, the absence of serious consultation as to staffing, training, and patient services is all too frequent.

Even where there is no intent to delude the public that with the reorganization of the courts social problems will be solved, this, too often, is the result. Recommendations by judicial bodies and bar associations may in time lead to some constructive steps. However, it is naive to expect members of such bodies to have either experience with or a sense of urgency about the problems of the inferior courts. Few of them have ever presided over or even visited courts dealing with social problems. They cannot comprehend the limitations imposed on judges who are given the responsibility to secure services without the authority to do so. As members of appellate bodies they are not torn by the dual obligation of fact-finding and of making dispositions without the resources to assure that their orders will not result in condemnation to further hurt rather than real help.

One illustration of such "progress" is to be found in the court reorganization in New York. Among other "reforms" it provided that incorrigible girls aged sixteen to eighteen should be transferred from the criminal courts to the new Family Court and treated as "persons in need of supervision." This so-called progressive step followed state-wide hearings by a legislative commission, bar association studies, and law school involvement, and had the support of social and civil agencies. However, there was no program for the study, treatment, or rehabilitation of the girls. As a result, when the law became effective in September, 1962, both the Department of Social Welfare and the Department of Correction held they were not responsible for providing care and treatment. There is still no residential facility which the court has the power to command.

The absence of treatment services throughout every area of court responsibility repeatedly reduces the social court to an institution that sanctions community neglect of the individual and so becomes the official executioner of his hopes and potential for change. To the extent that law and psychiatry are apathetic about such conditions, they condone them. All of us must heed the warning of Chief Justice Warren: "The poor who come to our social courts cannot survive in the modern world if progress continues at a snail's pace."[15]

[15] National Conference on Bail and Criminal Justice, *Proceedings 1964 and Interim Report, May 1964–April 1965* (Washington, D.C.: Office of the Attorney General, April, 1965).

For a long time the procedures used in social courts were largely ignored by the bar and appellate bench. The assumption that the juvenile courts were "non-criminal," together with the hope that they rehabilitated rather than punished the child led to state court decisions that approved informal hearings, the use of hearsay evidence, the absence of counsel, failure to keep written records, and even denial of the right of appeal. Closed to the public and the press, the social courts were also largely ignored by members of the bar, who rarely appeared there.[16]

Possibly stimulated by discoveries of what "due process" had been found *not* to mean for criminal defendants and for the mentally ill, the United States Supreme Court agreed to review the conviction of a minor by the Criminal Court of the District of Columbia, following waiver of jurisdiction by the Juvenile Court of the District.[17] When he was fourteen years old the defendant, Kent, was arrested and placed on probation as a result of several housebreakings and an attempted purse-snatching. Two years later he was taken into custody on the basis of fingerprints taken in the juvenile court at the time of his first offense. He was charged with entering an apartment, stealing a wallet, and raping the occupant. Although within the jurisdiction of the juvenile court because of his age, he was taken to police headquarters and interrogated for seven hours, removed to the detention home overnight and the next day again interrogated at police headquarters from morning until five in the afternoon. Counsel engaged by his mother filed a motion for hearing on the question of waiver of jurisdiction to the criminal court, submitting an affidavit by a psychiatrist and an offer of proof that, with adequate treatment in a hospital under the aegis of the juvenile court, the boy would be a suitable subject for rehabilitation. Counsel also moved to have the social service file of the court made available to him.

---

[16] Daniel L. Skoler and Charles W. Tenney, Jr., "Attorney Representation in Juvenile Courts," *Journal of Family Law*, IV (Spring, 1964), 77–98. A questionnaire directed to judges serving in the seventy-five largest cities of the nation and in a few other large jurisdictions disclosed that lawyers appeared on behalf of children in less than 5 per cent of delinquency cases.

[17] *Kent* v. *United States*, 383 U.S. 541 (1966).

The juvenile court judge neither ruled on these motions nor held a hearing. He did not confer with the boy, his parents, or his counsel. He entered an order stating that after full investigation he waived jurisdiction and directed that the boy be held for trial under the regular procedures of the United States District Court. He made no findings and gave no reasons for the waiver of jurisdiction. The defense of this boy in the criminal court was directed to proving that he was not criminally responsible, under the Durham rule, because "his unlawful act was the product of mental disease or defect." The jury found that on the six counts of housebreaking and robbery he was criminally responsible and guilty. He was sentenced to serve thirty to ninety years on these counts. However, as to the count alleging rape, the same jury found he was not guilty by reason of insanity. This finding under the law of the District of Columbia meant that he would be transferred to a mental institution until his sanity was restored.

The conviction was affirmed by the United States Court of Appeals for the District of Columbia.[18] In a concurring opinion, Judge George Washington wrote: "It is a fair inference from the record before us that one of the reasons why the Juvenile Court waived jurisdiction was because appellant was seriously disturbed and the Juvenile Court lacked facilities adequately to treat him." In a dissenting opinion, Chief Judge Bazelon rejoined: "I think it is shocking that a child was subjected to prosecution and punishment as a criminal because he was thought to suffer from a serious mental or emotional disturbance. I can think of no stronger reason for not doing this."

On review of this record the United States Supreme Court reversed the conviction, holding that the latitude allowed the juvenile court in regard to waiver of jurisdiction did "not confer upon the Juvenile Court a license for arbitrary procedure." The court pointed out the consequences of the transfer of a child to jail and a possible death sentence, instead of treatment for a maximum of five years until he reached the age of twenty-one, and demanded that the basic requirements of due process and fairness be observed. The Court held that such requirements

[18] 119 U.S. App. D.C. 395, 343 F.2d 264 (1964).

prohibited a decision to waive jurisdiction in isolation, without a hearing, without opening the court records to counsel, and without a statement of the reasons for waiving jurisdiction.

The opinion for the Court, delivered by Mr. Justice Fortas, expressed many concerns that went beyond the holding of the case. It referred to serious questions that had been raised in studies "as to whether the actual performance of the Juvenile Courts measure well enough against theoretical purpose to make tolerable the immunity of the process from the reach of the constitutional guarantees applicable to adults." This decision was singled out by Professor Archibald Cox as one of the highlights of the 1965 term, in that it moved away from treating procedural rights in criminal cases as not essential to proceedings designated as "civil." He saw this decision as properly focusing on the consequence of the proceedings to the defendant, and wrote that the Kent case left "little doubt that denial of important procedural safeguards in state courts will be subject to a serious attack on due process grounds."[19]

Within the space of a few months this prophecy was fulfilled by the decision of the United States Supreme Court in *In the Matter of Gault*.[20] In this case a child on probation to the juvenile court in Arizona was taken into custody charged with having used lewd language to a woman on the telephone. The child was questioned without notice to his mother and was then held in detention. He was not represented by counsel. The complaining witness was not brought to court, and her complaint was submitted by a probation officer. No transcript was made of the hearing, and the boy was committed to a state school until he was twenty-one years of age. In Arizona the state statute does not allow the right of appeal to the highest court.

The decision of the Supreme Court reversing the lower court's finding has been hailed as extending constitutional requirements of due process to the juvenile courts and as a harbinger of further judicial review of the substantive services provided by them. It has also been attacked by some who see it as a prelude

[19] "The Supreme Court 1965 Term," p. 127.
[20] 387 U.S. 1 (1967).

to reducing the juvenile court to a replica of the criminal courts, in which the welfare of the child will be submerged in adversary proceedings. The majority opinion delivered by Mr. Justice Fortas does not warrant either conclusion. It does hold that "neither the Fourteenth Amendment nor the Bill of Rights is for adults alone." It specifically establishes minimal procedural requirements at fact-finding hearings. It holds that: (1) notice of charges of delinquency must be given sufficiently in advance of scheduled court proceedings and must set forth the alleged misconduct with particularity and not in vague or general terms; (2) the assistance of counsel is essential for the determination of delinquency; (3) the constitutional privilege against self-incrimination is applicable to juveniles;[21] and (4) the testimony against a juvenile must be presented under oath and the opportunity for cross-examination must be made available, in accordance with the requirements of law and the Constitution.

In Professor Monrad Paulsen's judgment, "the *Gault* decision is built upon the premise that the juvenile court system has failed to provide the care and treatment that the theory underlying it had posited."[22] While dictum in the opinion of Mr. Justice Fortas in this case, as in the Kent case, clearly expresses concern about the disparity between the hopes for and the achievements of the juvenile courts, neither decision includes any findings or holdings on the question.

It is true that the opinion did refer to writings that underlined the gap between the rhetoric used regarding the juvenile court and the realities of court and institutional services. However, in the Kent case the Court specifically stated that it was not dealing with such basic issues, and in the Gault case the Court specifically stated that its findings were limited to the adjudicatory hearing and that it was not directing its attention to the dispositional process.

---

[21] In discussing the use of confessions, the majority opinion referred to the danger of official urging of confessions followed by disciplinary action. It spoke of the likelihood of a hostile reaction on the part of the child, who might feel tricked by being punished despite his confession. It also referred to the formidable doubt that has been cast upon the reliability of confessions by children.

[22] "Children's Court Gateway of Last Resort," *Columbia University Forum*, X, No. 2 (Summer, 1967), 4.

While the progress made in protecting the constitutional rights of the child in the adjudicatory process is to be welcomed, it will in no way compensate for the lack of dispositional remedies. *Gault* may protect some children from unfair hearings and wrongful findings, but it will not provide one dollar's worth of professional mental health services or one hour of care for any troubled child.

We are the heirs of over half a century of scientific search, parental concern, and lay interest in the relationship of child-rearing to adult behavior. Vocabularies have changed; customs or mores of child care have changed. There is widespread acknowledgment of the extent to which relationships between parent and child, between the parents, between teacher and child, and between the community and the family affect the lives of the individual and the family. Yet there has been reluctance to relate what we have learned from psychiatry to law, where decisions determine future relationships in families.

In an era of specialization, within the professional fields of sociology, psychology, education, anthropology, and psychiatry, many new subfields are concentrating on the problems of family life and the development of children. At the same time there is a widespread assumption that anyone and everyone can be an expert on children, on their treatment when they become delinquent, and on matters of custody and care. For the most part the specialists are regarded as a mop-up squad essential only if the label of either physical or mental illness is first attached to the child. The notion that anyone can be an expert also extends to the treatment of adults. Only recently J. Edgar Hoover cited an ex-convict as his authority for the doctrine that longer sentences serve as a deterrent to crime, since "only fear keeps people in line."

While intensive and expensive research is pursued in some aspects of family life and child care, the vast majority of dependent, neglected, and delinquent children and troubled families are handled by untrained staff in public welfare departments, courts, and institutions. In this country the idea that a judge who decides on the removal of a child from his family, on custody questions, or on adoption should have special training has hardly been considered. In addition, the absence of adequate professional advice and services forces a role upon the judge for which no brief training could prepare him.

In the juvenile courts children and parents have generally not been represented by counsel. When they are so represented, it is usually not by counsel adequately trained to protect their legal rights and secure the most effective service for them. For the most part, commitment of a child for psychiatric observation is based on either uncontrollable or bizarre action in the court or on evidence of misconduct that seems threatening to the community. In the absence of immediate psychiatric consultation, many children are subjected by the courts to unnecessary hospitalization, and others whose symptoms are not so obvious are denied such observation when it might be most beneficial.

In the various divisions of the family courts that have jurisdiction over non-support, orders of visitation, and simple assaults within the home, husband and wife are usually not represented by counsel. In such emotionally charged situations and in the absence of psychiatric consultation, judges are inevitably reluctant to use the power of hospital commitment except in cases of extreme acting-out behavior. Experience with many cases in which charges of grave misconduct and even violence by husband or wife have been followed by reconciliation of the couple have made judges skeptical about reports of threats of violence without other substantiating evidence. Charges and counter-charges are the order of the day. At times it seems as though the judge, generally of middle-class background, comes to regard threats and violence as the way of life of those who come from a low socioeconomic background. The court, like the police, is less ready to intervene in family quarrels among "the poor."

The court is reluctant to deprive a man of his freedom, especially when his work record is good and the man denies the aggressive or even bizarre conduct alleged. Conventional and traditional beliefs about the family also weigh the scales against hospital commitment of a spouse. Husbands and wives, despite mutually destructive conduct toward one another and even in the presence of indications of serious psychopathology, are often lectured by the judge on their marriage vows and the importance of family unity and are told "to make up and try again." How such moralistic courtroom lectures affect the docile or aggressive member of the family would provide an interesting study. However, it has become quite evident that the satisfaction felt by the judge that his lecture has "saved a family" is often misplaced. At times it has even caused grave tragedies affecting both the parents and their children.

Without adequate legal counsel to present all the facts and without the help of psychiatric consultation, the judge is forced to rely on his intuition, his superficial and swift probing of the family relationship, and his personal value system, derived in large part from his religious upbringing and cultural background. In this, as in many other areas of human and social problems, the absence of follow-up studies to determine the results of actual practices leaves open a wide area for argument, theorizing, and position-taking that are unrelated to the realities of life. The gathering of a body of knowledge from which judges might learn should lead to a modification of the present hit-or-miss practices now employed when the disputing parties have no substantial financial means. Follow-up studies of what actually happens to husbands, wives and children under the present practices are desperately needed as a basis for considering both how law and psychiatry can contribute to strengthening the family and when pathology requires that a family be separated.

In observing law and psychiatry in action in the family court, I have been constantly struck by the divergent role which each plays and the curious way in which each is viewed by the other. Sometimes it seems as though the blind spots are caused by the limited focus of interest on the part of a judge or psychiatrist. At other times judges and psychiatrists seem totally unaware of each other's function, even to the point of disregard, if not contempt, for that function. One witnesses cases in court where denial of visitation privileges to an erring father, whether alcoholic, drug-addicted, engaged in an illicit affair, or non-supporting, reflects a censorious judgment. Exclusion or even limitation of future contact with children is used as a form of punishment, although it may be disguised in such terms as "the best interest of the child."

The law, through the courts, is likely to add stress to the interpersonal relations between husbands and wives and husbands and children by entering support orders that make even a modest existence impossible for the father or husband who has left the home. Here the heritage of the criminal law—the punishment of the deserting breadwinner—is supported by the tradition of the Elizabethan poor laws, which were intended to save the taxpayer money at all costs. Also, sympathy for the abandoned wife and children and judgmental attitudes toward the husband and father provoke orders of support that may well impose such hardship as to drain away both a sense of guilt and of responsibility toward his wife and children. The subsequent defaults, defiance, or disappearance of the father are far from helpful to anyone concerned. In other situations, where the mother's conduct either shocks the judge or is inconsistent with his views as to the duty of a wife to remain with her husband for "better or for worse," the exercise of judicial discretion through a niggardly order of support becomes the unacknowledged lash of punishment.

The courts are constantly confronted by human beings who have already suffered from the lack of psychiatric services prior to their court appearance. The problems thus created add to the persistent distrust of psychiatry by the courts. In addition, the apparent failure of psychiatrists to give practical help in meeting the serious problems that confront the courts adds to the distrust. Repeatedly, where a husband is alcoholic, a narcotics addict, or anti-social and is committed for observation after acts of abuse or threats to kill, a hospital will find that he is "not psychotic" and therefore not committable and will return him to the custody of the court. No practicable advice is given by hospital authorities, and no concern is shown for the other members of the family. Illustrations of such situations are numberless. Two small children were returned to a mother on her release from a state hospital, only to be brought before the court six months after her discharge from aftercare as having been physically abused for the second time. No arrangement had been made upon her discharge for supervision of the children to protect them against an acute recurrence of her illness. Contrary to the clinical insights that abound in the psychiatric literature, in cases such as this one finds the psychiatric reports from the physician who has treated the mother or father to be concerned solely with the adult patient. The children, if mentioned, rarely seem to be known to the physician treating the adult and are too often seen only as good or bad medicine for the adult's recovery. The consequences for the children returned to such parents, in terms of their mental health, are rarely explored.

The court receives reports from psychiatrists who have treated a mentally ill mother or father, who, when the acute episode is over (at least temporarily), recommend extensive visitation and even custody of their children as "good therapy" for the patient. The absence of any real contact with the other parent and the children and the lack of concern for the effect of the patient's illness on the other members of the family make such recommendations appear to be focused only on the patient. When there is a long history of family difficulties or conflicts, such recommendations for family "togetherness" seem as untherapeutic as do the moralistic punishments imposed by the court in its support orders and restriction of visitation rights.

In a case heard some months ago an excellent psychiatric institution recommended that a mother who had been hospitalized several times and was then attending its out-patient clinic on a monthly basis while receiving chemotherapy could care for her three little girls, aged six, nine, and twelve. When the children were seen in court chambers, they told the presiding judge that their mother had been burning candles, believed God was showing her where she would find things that had been misplaced, and woke the children at night to discuss her youthful sexual misconduct and to ask whether it would not be best to end her life and theirs. Despite reports of this conduct to her psychiatrist, he felt that she would not injure the children and that she showed some improvement. He saw no need for action to protect the children, nor did he feel it necessary to see them to evaluate what was happening before recommending continuing custody in the mother. His sole concern was that the mother might "break" again if the children were removed.

In community psychiatry, great stress is placed on widening the psychiatrist's knowledge so that he may delegate some of his responsibility to other child care or family care professions. In doing so, it is recognized that in many cases the removal or reduction of environmental stresses may provide the means to mental health. Yet this approach seems all too rarely embraced by the psychiatrist in recommendations concerning patients discharged or paroled by state hospitals. Little stress is placed on the family pathology to which the patient is returned or on the need for changing living arrangements to prevent further illness. Here, again, the focus of the psychiatrist's attention seems too narrow.

In an illuminating paper on training for community psychiatry, Dr. Viola Bernard expresses the view that "the community psychiatrist must be able to stretch his accustomed capacity for identifying with one single person into a capacity for the simultaneous maintenance of multiple identifications. . . . the psychological interests and needs of many members of the population which he serves are often in conflict with each other."[23]

Without demanding as much of the psychiatrists in the clinic, the extension of out-patient treatment to the person who has experienced many family and social problems also requires that they make an effort to understand such problems to a degree beyond that required for the private practitioner, whose patients' family members can secure help individually. For most families, even those above the strict poverty line, the acceptance of one member for treatment gives no assurance that any of the helping professions will become involved with rendering aid to the other members. The good fortune of one person in reaching a port of psychiatric entry may thus lead to injury to his family and eventually to himself if he is never seen in the family context and if the welfare of other family members is not a matter of concern to his psychiatrist.

---

[23] Viola W. Bernard, M.D., *Some Aspects of Training for Community Psychiatry in a University Medical Center* (U.S. Department of Health, Education, and Welfare Public Health Society Publication No. 1319; Washington, D.C.: Government Printing Office, 1965), pp. 65–66.

Lack of responsibility for follow-up or follow-through is characteristic of lawyers and psychiatrists under present procedures. There is a remarkable similarity between the pretensions of psychiatry and of law in their after-care programs for patients and for defendants following confinement. Though both hail after-care as of utmost importance in progress toward rehabilitation and in learning the use of freedom, in practice neither has provided substantial help. A neglected or delinquent child removed from his home and placed in an institution is somehow expected, on his return to the same inadequate home and slum, to make a good adjustment to school and the streets as well as to his family. In similar fashion, a child who has been confined to a state hospital and diagnosed as mentally ill is expected, upon release from the hospital, to maintain his drug therapy, return to school, and adjust to the family in which he became ill, all with little help.

Unrealistic expectations on the part of the psychiatric profession as to what the law can do through the courts reflect the lack of joint planning and cooperation on behalf of mentally ill or emotionally disturbed parents and their children. Its diagnostic pronouncements, including recognition of potential danger, leave the courts with full responsibility for threatening situations but no way to protect the family or community. Such diagnoses can only add to the court's anxiety and sense of helplessness and frustration.

Thus the father of four children ranging in age from four to twelve was brought before a family court for excessive drinking, failure to support the family, and abusiveness to the mother when drinking. He was hospitalized for observation and returned to court two weeks later. The psychological report stated he was a weak, immature, and passively dependent personality who attempted to manipulate his environment without being able to accept responsibility. The hospital found no evidence that he was clinically psychotic but added that under the influence of alcohol he was capable of acting in a bizarre manner. The psychiatric examiner stated that when the patient was sober he was in good contact, pleasant, and functioned fairly well. He added, however, that when under the influence of drink the patient became quite disturbed and "loses most of his controls and becomes dangerous." The diagnosis followed: "Schizoid personality; chronic alcoholism. He is not committable nor would any purpose be served by committing him. He should be encouraged to get some out-patient treatment for his alcoholism. . . . He should remain under the supervision of the court." The final sentence adds insult to utter frustration for the court. How can the court protect these children from danger when the father becomes drunk? How, with a case load of sixty to one hundred children per probation officer, can the court supervise this man, described as a schizoid chronic alcoholic? How can it prevent him from becoming intoxicated, get him into treatment, or induce him to accept responsibility?

In another case in which the father had admitted abuse of his wife and five children, the hospital returned him to the court as not overtly psychotic and not committable at this time, along with a diagnosis: "schizophrenic reaction, paranoid type. . . . He shows little insight and no capacity for responsibility and is obsessed with enormous feelings of inferiority." Then the psychiatric report added, with a flourish that the court could only regard as a washing of medical hands, "Since we feel that there is abundant evidence that the patient is extremely aggressive and possibly homicidal, we would recommend that the court take such precautions as are necessary to protect his wife and family. . . . While psychotherapy might be of help, the patient resists such treatment. We would suggest that it be recommended when he is ready to accept it."

The courts are perplexed by such reports. Composed of laymen educated to some psychiatric insights, they know that swift and temporary imprisonment is no answer. Yet when the courts do reach out for psychiatric help, the responsibility is often not only tossed back upon them, but tossed back along with recommendations that are unrealistic. The hospitals are all but saying that they can do nothing, that the situation is potentially dangerous, and that the responsibility rests with the courts.

Psychiatrists' parallel experiences with the law must also give them a similar sense of hopelessness and frustration. The abuse of lay judgment to the point at which life is endangered despite full warning by physicians results when judges override clear recommendations for commitment of an adult or child found to be psychotic. A little girl nearly eleven years old was brought before a juvenile court by her mother as in need of supervision. The mother, fearful because she had previously been charged with neglect of her five out-of-wedlock children, hesitantly explained that her daughter had tried to set fire to an infant sister. Hospital observation of the child was ordered by the court. Psychiatrists found the child subject to frequent auditory hallucinations and alternating between withdrawn conduct and impulsive assaultive outbursts: "A man's voice tells me hit your sister"—another voice "tells me not to." The doctors warned that with her history and symptoms the child could become a homicidal risk and required further hospitalization. The judge disagreed, and the child was released to the mother pending a return appearance in the juvenile court. In the intervening few days the mother found her daughter with a chair in her hands, about to smash her infant sister. The court asked the mother what the hospital had said when the child was released. She reported having been told that "She's not crazy and I should take her home." In her hand she held the mimeographed form from the psychiatric division. The first paragraph stated that in the opinion of the psychiatrists the child should be placed in a state hospital. The next paragraph stated that the supreme court justice who had heard the case had ordered that the child be discharged from the hospital and had given the opinion that the child was not mentally ill. The third paragraph stated that since the child was still under the jurisdiction of the juvenile term, the mother was ordered to take the child back to court. Beneath these confusing statements was a separate paragraph in which the mother had to acknowledge that she had been directed and would obey the order to take the child back to juvenile court. On questioning the mother, it was learned that she had been given no warning of the danger to her other children. On a call to the hospital, the juvenile court judge was advised that despite certification by two doctors that the child was mentally ill the supreme court justice had refused to commit the child and had discharged her to the mother. The child was returned to the hospital, not for further observation but to await the advent of another judge who would listen to psychiatric findings.

Even in urban areas, where some psychiatric expertise is available to the courts, it has been largely restricted to inadequate diagnoses in the juvenile courts (mostly serving the poor) and to "expert testimony" submitted by the battling parents in custody proceedings (serving the more affluent). Systematic use or pursuit of knowledge helpful in determining what decision would be most likely to give the child the greatest opportunity for healthy development is largely absent. Legal statutes and decisions clothe procedures and conclusions in the phrase "the best interest of the child," a phrase that has little relationship to the realities of life.

It is interesting that in Europe, where analytic work concerning children was first developed, juvenile courts had contact with workers in this field over thirty years ago, but even there the contacts were temporary and lacked continuity.[24] A few years ago Anna Freud stated that the first systematic scrutiny of psychoanalytic teachings and data as applicable to the problems of children presented to courts was only then being undertaken at the Yale University Law School. In her seminars at Yale and elsewhere she spoke of analytic knowledge concerning the harmful effects of the separation of a child from a mother or father and the relevance of a child's age to evaluation of these effects. She spoke of loyalty conflicts and the child's ability to tolerate them as factors to be considered in the determination of rights of visitation. Clinical analyses of the relationship between parental disturbance and the subsequent neurotic, psychotic, or delinquent pathology of children were presented as possible guides for warranting intervention by the court as a preventive measure. Studies of the differing effects on the social adaptation of children to various types of discipline, including corporal punishment, were seen as relevant to decision making in regard to both custody and supervision by courts.

[24] See August Aichorn, *Wayward Youth* (New York: Viking Press, 1935).

Other available data and studies were suggested by Miss Freud as guides in regard to the removal of children from their own homes and for child care practices. These included assessment of the traumatic impact on children of criminal events in the family and knowledge of the psychological harm resulting from placement in multiple foster homes.

After reading many case records from American courts, Miss Freud expressed the opinion that the biggest contribution to be made might be to construct a revised definition of what is in the "best interest of the child." In her view:

> the best interests of a child are served . . . by all measures which promote his smooth progression toward normal maturity. The latter, in turn, depends above all on the coincidence of three factors; on the free interchange of affection between child and adult, on ample external stimulation of the child's inborn internal potentialities; and on unbroken continuity of care.[25]

Unfortunately, the studies and data referred to by Anna Freud as possible guidelines for the courts in determining questions of custody, visitation, or removal of a child because of neglect are rarely known to members of the judiciary or to its auxiliary personnel. If known, to what extent such data would be acceptable to persons trained in law, who often see themselves as arbiters of the morals and mores of the community and who are largely governed by their own religious and cultural loyalties, is debatable. There is the additional problem which Miss Freud recognized: the "child psychologists and also child analysts are out of touch frequently with work in the practical fields or offer the knowledge which they possess in forms which preclude its direct application to the services in schools, nurseries, residential homes, hospitals, children's courts, etc."[26]

There is probably no area in which law and psychiatry have had and may continue to have a greater opportunity to complement each other in service than through the juvenile or family courts, yet promise and practice remain worlds apart. In search-

---

[25] Psychoanalytic Knowledge of the Child and Its Application to Children's Services," p. 20.

[26] *Ibid.*, pp. 5–6.

ing for the reasons, one can escape neither the conceptual conflicts between law and psychiatry nor the limitations of court personnel, including judges, probation officers, and court psychiatrists. However, a far more basic impediment to the fulfillment of the promise derives from unrealistic expectations. It is assumed that a court, like the little Dutch boy, can put its thumb in the dike and by an order hold back the sea of troubles that have submerged, or threaten to submerge, those who come before it. Like other feats of engineering built on inadequate foundations or with skills not yet sufficient to the task, the courts require re-examination and reinforcement if they are to become useful and functional structures.

Judicial decisions following battles between parents for custody of children rarely give evidence of adequate help from the psychiatric profession in evaluating the effects of separation on children, their conflict in loyalties, or their emotional needs at different stages in their development. Contrary to English tradition, which bestowed on the father an all but absolute right to custody, the presumption in this country is that children, especially if very young, should reside with their mothers. The rebuttal of this presumption is based too often not on the welfare of the child but on a further unspoken premise that the determination of custody should reward innocence or punish "immoral conduct." This premise emerges in particularly pronounced fashion where publicity accompanies a court trial.

In a famous custody case, the trial judge granted a divorce to a husband on the grounds of adultery but gave custody to the wife because the record showed a long history of marital conflict due to the husband's inadequacy as a father, the great love between the mother and two daughters, aged thirteen and eleven, and their unhappiness when forced to be with their father. On appeal the highest court in the state reversed the decision with an opinion that placed stress on the fact that there was "neither proof nor claim that the defendant [mother] has repented." The highest court stated that its decision as to custody "cannot be one repugnant to all normal concepts of sex, family and marriage." In a dissent, one judge took the position that the trial court was in far the better position to make a decision and that the paramount concern of the trial judge had properly been the welfare and the happiness of the children.

There are rare custody cases where one finds the happy combination of opposing lawyers who join forces to help parents place the welfare of their children first and of a judge whose knowledgeable concern for the children causes him to search, with the help of expert psychiatric advice, for the answer in terms of their healthy development. In one such case, where a father brought a writ of *habeas corpus* against his wife to secure custody of the children, a child psychiatrist was selected by the court to make an independent evaluation of what would be best for them. It was agreed by counsel for both parties that the psychiatrist should recommend whatever would be most likely to correct or alleviate the children's problems. Counsel for the parents agreed that both would be available and would cooperate in the study. All previous medical reports on the parents were to be made available to the psychiatrist. The parents were seen with and without the children, and the children were seen separately. A home visit with the mother and observation of the children before and after a stay with the father were made.

The resulting report concluded that the father was by far the healthier of the two parents and that the pervasive emotional problems of the mother made it impossible for her to be the kind of mother that intellectually she would wish to be. It was found that the mother's problems spilled over onto the children, preventing normal emotional growth, creating serious anxiety, and depriving them intellectually and emotionally. Improvement in the children while with the father was noted, as was his ability to accept help and to both plan and carry through wholesome planning for them. As a result of this report, together with other testimony, the court granted custody to the father and directed supervised visitation with the mother pending the beginning of her psychiatric treatment. Substantial funds were needed for medical and legal fees and for ongoing treatment for the mother and the children, which the father was ready and able to provide. Such a happy combination of circumstances is unusual.

As one reads the record in this case, one additional element is significant. Great emphasis was placed on the development of the children and on the need for reviewing their development and needs as they grew older. This procedure contrasts with the general practice of securing diagnostics at a particular moment and drawing conclusions based on the assumption that what is good for children at one stage in their lives will continue to be so throughout their minority.[27]

In the vast proportion of cases where a divorce is not contested, the question of the welfare of children, in terms of which parent has more to offer to their healthy development, is not considered by the court. The plaintiff, generally the wife, sets forth in legal language whatever the state statute requires to secure a divorce (whether adultery, cruelty, or incompatibility). The allegations are not denied by the father, who is often the one actually seeking the divorce. The divorce is granted, and the children automatically go to the plaintiff as benefits or burdens go with land that is sold. The pre-divorce agreement between the parties may or may not reflect concern for the welfare of the children. The primary interest of one party in escaping the marriage, or financial considerations unrelated to the soundness of the custody or visitation agreements, control the disposition of the children. The mental health of the respective parents, past anti-social behavior, and their ability to be parents are not subjected to scrutiny.

Unfortunately, there have been no follow-up studies to throw light on whether such parental agreements produce results that

[27] See Anna Freud, *Normality and Pathology in Childhood, Assessments of Development* (New York: International Universities Press, 1965), pp. 109–10. Miss Freud acknowledges that the demarcation line between mental health and illness, which has caused so much trouble for both lawyers and psychiatrists, is "even more difficult to draw in childhood than in later stages." The uneven rate of growth, temporary or permanent repressions, and other factors provide a constantly shifting picture of the development of the child, so as to increase the confusing aspects of the clinical picture. While the child analyst has as yet stopped short of the classification of disorder, the "whole psychopathology of childhood has been fitted, more or less forcibly, into the existing diagnostic categories taken over wholesale not only from the field of adult analysis, but from adult psychiatry and criminology." To Miss Freud, "this solution of the diagnostic question proves unsatisfactory as a basis for assessment, prognosis and selection of therapeutic measures."

in the long run are better or worse for their children than those that result from court decisions following custody battles. The lack of study may reflect over-confidence in the "natural rights" of parents to keep or separate themselves from their children, the uneasiness of the state about becoming further involved in family matters, and the absence of sufficient concern for the welfare of the growing army of children of divorce.

In cases where the contest for custody is between a parent and a non-parent, the courts have repeatedly regarded the natural rights of the parents as superior to the best interest of the child. Jacobus ten Brock has written that in such cases the courts

> subordinated the independent judicial determination of the children's best interests, and developed the principle that the child is a chattel. . . . Contemporary cases speak of the natural right of the parent in the same way that earlier cases spoke of the property right, exalting the right and subordinating the duty, referring to the right almost in the Lockean sense of natural rights with overtones of absoluteness and inalienability.[28]

The widespread acceptance of the "inalienability of natural rights," even when it is not articulated, is also a factor in leaving children in situations of serious neglect and denying them opportunities for a normal and happy childhood in a substitute family. This assumption is present in legal pronouncements, in judicial action or non-action, and in the consistent failure of administrative agencies to seek removal of children from destructive family situations. In the recent American Bar Foundation study, cited several times previously, the statutory authorization, in thirty-eight states, to consider for non-consensual adoptions children whose parents are mentally disabled is referred to as a real danger if adoption is allowed in situations where the parents suffer from curable psychoses and the parent-child relationship may thus be unjustifiably severed.[29] Nothing is said of the

---

[28] See Jacobus ten Brock, "California's Dual System of Family Law: Its Origin, Development and Present Status," *Stanford Law Review*, XVI, Nos. 2 and 4 (March–July, 1964), 920–23, 925.

[29] *The Mentally Disabled and the Law*, p. 204. See *People* ex rel. *Nalstedt* v. *Barger*, 3 Ill.2d 511, 121 N.E.2d 781 (1954).

far more real danger to the many thousands of children retained in custodial care throughout their minority while their psychotic parents are permitted to maintain their "natural rights."

Contrary to what one might logically expect, children whose parents abandon them, neglect them, or are incapable of providing good care are also those most neglected by law, psychiatry, and our social agencies. They are the most likely to be overlooked. Because they do not present any immediate threat to the community through delinquent action, they are least likely to be referred for diagnostic studies. They are the most likely to be left in neglectful homes, where the damage to their growth is neither modified nor reversed. They are the most likely to remain in temporary shelters and custodial institutions for long periods of their young lives. Their docility and submission seem to invite further neglect by all concerned. Active help to terminate parental rights, to secure substitute homes, or to find adoptive homes runs aground on the shoals of apathy, the assumption that the agencies are providing such care as is in the best interest of the child, and dogmatic support of the "natural rights" of parents who are parents only in biological terms.

Despite verbal emphasis placed on the value of early recognition of mental health problems in children and work with their parents, preventive services are rarely available for the neglected child. When the situation becomes so acute that he must be removed from his home, the child himself does receive care, but services to improve the home situation so that the child may return to it are rarely provided.

In the juvenile courts one finds a greater proportion of referrals for diagnostic study of delinquent children than of neglected children. When a probation officer requests a psychiatric study of a neglected child because of serious problems, such a study is rarely followed by study of younger sisters and brothers unless they, too, show overt signs of disturbance. In order to spare neglected children court appearances, they are not brought before the court except in unusual cases, such as those of sexual molestation or physical abuse. The court is, therefore, likely to center attention on the offending adult rather than on the effects of the home situation on the child or children. Repeatedly our courts remove one child after another from a family when they become old enough to run away, become truant, or cause trouble in the community. It is only in the most extreme cases, despite serious family pathology, that preventive measures are taken to study and, if necessary, remove younger siblings.

Our guidance clinics, like the juvenile courts, while paying lip service to the importance of early identification and treatment, have failed to take the steps necessary to implement this policy. As Dr. Peter Neubauer has pointed out, explanations that only older children are referred, that the establishment of a clear diagnosis is difficult, that the staff is not trained to treat the preschool child, and that there are not enough professional treatment hours available are "little more than attempts to avoid the exposure of our own failure." His answer is that "we must move from giving services only to those who ask for help, to helping those who need it." He adds: "We can speak of a lack of referral only if we expect the large number of children with early and crippling emotional disorders to find us."[30]

The gap between tomes on child care, professional papers, and theoretically accepted standards and the actual treatment of poor children is so vast that both law and psychiatry stand all but helpless before the massive problems to be undertaken. Bad habits, apathy, lack of personnel, and lack of funds continue to prevent the implementation of known health-saving procedures. Like the denial of civil rights and the widespread unawareness of the injury to the individuals involved, the persistent denial of

---

[30] Peter B. Neubauer, M.D., "On the Neglect of the Young Child," *American Journal of Orthopsychiatry*, XXXIII, No. 5 (October, 1963), 777–78. In England the experience of the war years convinced Anna Freud of the urgent need for trained child therapists. Her previous experience had already shown her that many later psychological abnormalities could be prevented if the problems of psychological development could be studied and dealt with in early childhood. At the Well Baby Clinic for normal infants in Hampstead, in addition to providing help, the staff has tried to determine the limits within which guidance may serve to relieve important tensions as they arise between mother and child at this early stage. See the Anna Freud Foundation, "Report on the Hampstead Child Therapy Course & Clinic" (manuscript).

good child services to the poor has created an Augean stable which will require a monumental long-term effort to analyze and rectify. The development of foster care families to provide for children who are abandoned by or removed from their natural parents was long regarded as an ideal solution. In more recent years there is growing recognition that unless the child so removed is placed in a home that offers continuity of care and adults who love and are loved by the child, where he can sink his roots, the results may prove disastrous. Studies have shown that, once removed from his own family, the child is less and less likely to be returned to his natural parents as time passes and that constant shifting from home to home endangers the growth— the mental and the emotional health—of the child.

In one case a baby was born in prison to a mentally ill and defective mother, and the child's life history dramatizes what we do *to* rather than *for* such a child. She had been placed at birth in the infant ward of the prison, where she remained for fourteen months. There a single nurse cared for forty such infants. Placement in eight different foster homes followed during the first eight years of her life. By then a troubled child, she was transferred to an institution where she was in contact with a succession of fourteen different social workers during the next eight years. As one reads her story with its tragic development of irreversible maladjustment, it presents the necessity for re-examining what passes for "child care" and what is condoned and authorized by law.[31]

One is reminded of the legend of the ancient king who was determined to discover whether, if children were not taught any language, they would naturally speak Greek or Hebrew. He therefore ordered that a group of infants be removed from their natural parents and placed with nurses. The nurses were instructed to feed and care for them but not to speak to them or in their presence. The legend tells that the experiment could not be completed because none of the infants survived. As one reads the histories of children moved through hospitals, shelters,

[31] See Viola W. Bernard, M.D., "Community Health Programing," *Journal of the American Academy of Child Psychiatry*, IV, No. 2 (April, 1965), 226–37.

institutions, and a succession of foster care placements, one is forced to ask whether, even if they survive physically, we like the ancient king have not killed their capacity to relate to other human beings.

The absence of overt cruelty, the lack of drama, and the general lack of public concern makes the penetration of this curtain of cold cruelty all the more difficult. When eight neglected children ranging from one to fifteen years of age are distributed like rations among four different agencies wherever beds happen to be available, the law which sanctions such placements, the mental health organizations which are silent, the administrators of the law who condone the act, and the social agencies which provide such care are all partners in the offense against the children. The neglectful mother is silenced by her own failures. The law guardian, even if available, is not able to provide sound placement. Bed spaces command, and the children, with their loneliness and inability to speak, are passed about like so many pieces of merchandise to those who may attempt to give them kindly care but who will surely fail to provide any secure or cohesive family life.

There is a tragic failure on the part of voluntary agencies and public departments to strengthen family life, despite slogans, or to find substitute care which will provide any sense of permanent belonging, any sense of identity, for the child abandoned or neglected. Courts required to review placements of neglected children so as to protect their rights and assure public payment for their care discover that many children have been in foster care agencies for years after their abandonment by their natural parents with no positive action taken in all that time to find homes for them. This situation is especially common if the child is non-white. Passed from foster home to foster home or kept in institutions if they cause no trouble, these lost children become increasingly incapable of loving or attaching themselves deeply to anyone. Reaching out, they have too frequently been rebuffed, or the loved one has disappeared too often to be again replaced by another new figure. The plight of two such children was brought to the attention of one family court when the state department of welfare instituted an action for support from responsible relatives. On inquiry by the court, it was learned that the children had not been visited by a relative for six years but that no action to secure a permanent substitute home had been taken on their behalf either by the agency caring for them or by the department of welfare.

Too often the courts have permitted themselves to become actors in a ceremony of official approval for whatever is being done or left undone for neglected children. Without sufficient or qualified staff to discover the needs of and the possibilities for children placed with foster care agencies, the voluminous files loom larger than the child. The court is not made aware of the separation of siblings, the failure to work with the parents, and the failure to institute legal action on behalf of the child to free him for adoption and is given only a brief statement on why the child should be continued in placement.[32] The lack of appropriate service by the social agencies, thus sanctioned and subsidized by court action, condemns countless children to emotionally arid lives. In one case a mother's whereabouts had been unknown since 1961, when her child, then an infant, had been placed in a foster care agency because of neglect. For four years no action had been taken to secure termination of parental rights in order to free the child for adoptive placement. In another case where the child had been placed three years earlier, first in an institution and then in a temporary foster home, extension of placement was likewise requested, although the father had died and the mother had disappeared over a year before the court hearing. Again nothing had been done to find a permanent home, and no developmental studies that would give the court an adequate picture of the child and his needs had accompanied the request for approving further public support.

[32] On one day in New York County in 1965 the Family Court calendar included twenty cases in which agencies requested extension of placement. No information was available concerning siblings in other agencies or in the home. In some instances, on inquiry by the court, it was found that siblings were scattered among as many as three or four agencies and that there was no information about how they were getting along. Nothing was known about plans for getting the siblings together or even for plans to arrange visiting each other.

In testimony before Congress in 1962, Joseph H. Reid[33] urged increased federal funds for child welfare services in order to raise the low standard of care for the two million children of this generation who would live part of their lives in some form of foster care. He cited the national study of foster care of children done by the Child Welfare League of America in 1959,[34] which found that (1) up to one half of children in foster care are there needlessly and should be placed for adoption or returned to their own homes; (2) fewer than 20 per cent of the parents of children in foster care are working with the foster care agency either toward rehabilitation of their homes or toward making other homes for the children; (3) of the children in foster care 50 per cent showed severe emotional disturbances; (4) more than 25 per cent of these children had been placed in at least four different foster homes; and (5) if the child has been in foster care for eighteen months or more, there is a strong probability he will remain there for the rest of his childhood.

Mr. Reid's testimony, based on years of professional studies of the actual conditions in which such children live, points to several areas where there is urgent need for psychiatric services, both preventive and therapeutic. The need of therapy for the 50 per cent of the children who show signs of serious emotional disturbances is obvious. It is equally clear that a sound mental health approach must be developed that will work more effectively with parents whose children have been placed in foster care because of neglect, so that these children will not spend their childhood going from one foster care placement to another.

Adoption agencies which provide the unmarried mother with comprehensive services, including psychiatric help, have shown what can be done to help girls to surrender children for whom

---

[33] Executive Director of the Child Welfare League of America, testimony presented February 13, 1962. Mr. Reid noted that only 50 per cent of the counties in the United States have child care workers (testimony in support of House Report 10032).

[34] *Children in Need of Parents* (New York: Columbia University Press, 1959). In the same testimony Mr. Reid supported the provision of federal funds to stimulate day care services, a suggestion that has since been enacted into law. He urged the necessity of such services for hundreds of thousands of children left without parental protection during significant parts of the day and of the importance of this service to prevent the breaking up of homes and the unnecessary placement of children in foster care.

they can neither provide or make sound future plans. It has also been shown that the taking of a child from the unmarried mother without therapeutic services to help her resolve her conflicts leaves her bruised and often permanently troubled.

Appropriate community services for the mother who feels she must work or wishes to while her children are still young, the screening out of mothers who wish to remain at home, and the provision of special services for working mothers are still minimal. Old dogmas about the mother's duty to remain at home have delayed the recognition that many working mothers can provide a more wholesome home for their children than they could if they were tethered to the house and dependent on public assistance. Even in the 1930's, the depression days, one frequently found the mother who secured work, who was determined not to live on the "dole," a far better homemaker than the martyred, deprived mother who had given up hope and was relying on inadequate public assistance. It has taken thirty years for us to see clearly what some mental health experts, some social workers, and some community planners have been urging on those who make laws, control the pursestrings, and can prevent change.

The records of the juvenile and criminal courts demonstrate that the delinquent adolescent and the young criminal have usually never had homes in which they received wholesome love or good nurturing. They are yesterday's neglected children on whose behalf the community failed to act. Surely the reading of the biographies of both Lee Harvey Oswald and Jack Ruby, which I cited earlier in another context, should have shocked this country out of its complacency about the failure to intervene on behalf of neglected children, if only to demonstrate the danger to the community that follows from such non-intervention. Without going into the details of their lives, it should be recalled that at the trial Dr. Manfred Guttmacher gave a brief history of Ruby's family background. He noted that the father was a drunken tyrant and the mother an ineffectual woman who was a certified paranoiac. From the ages of seven to fifteen Ruby had been in half a dozen different foster homes.[35]

[35] Guttmacher, *The Mind of the Murderer*, pp. 12–13.

In his discussion of the case Dr. Guttmacher stated: "one can safely hypothesize that the amount of satisfying nurture that the child receives in its earliest years must be a fundamental element in the formation of attitudes on the value of human life."[36] If this be so, the challenge to psychiatry as well as to lawmakers goes far beyond the provision of preventive services for the potential criminal or delinquent. The question raised is of how far our society shall be concerned that satisfying nurture be provided by natural parents, how far it is ready to buttress the inadequate parent, and how far it is prepared to intervene and provide the best supplementary or substitute forms of nurture when parents cannot or will not provide a healthy home.

Cases of "neglect" continue to be seen in the juvenile court, now with a new label—"hard-core neglect," a phrase used to justify society's failure to provide help for the children involved when it was first needed. Thus when one child was brought before the court as in need of supervision because of truancy and minor misconduct, a call to the New York City Department of Welfare revealed that the department was not handling the case. Insistence on a report on the case finally elicited the fact that the mother had been known to the department for eighteen years. She had had nine children out of wedlock by seven fathers, most of whom were only casual acquaintances. One child had drowned in the bathtub and five had been sent to various relatives in the Midwest over the past fourteen years and had never been visited by the mother. The home was found in disarray when visited, and the mother's interest in the children was reported to be limited. She appeared unaware of her responsibilities and overwhelmed by the situation. The report concluded that no worker had ever indicated the need for placement of the children, and that the case was not acceptable to the unit that provided special counseling services "because it is considered a hard core case."

Within the category of neglected children are those left in unfit homes without any effort made to intervene or modify the

[36] Quoted in Sybille Bedford, "The Ruby Case," *Life Magazine*, LVI, No. 36–36B (February 28, 1964).

pathology of the home situation until it becomes so critical that they must be removed. Then, although they should be placed in a foster home or in group care, children with sisters and brothers are separated and placed wherever vacancies are found. Under an interstate compact or agreement they may even be denied the opportunity to live with concerned relatives in another state unless there is an undertaking that they will not become public charges.[37]

At times the measures taken to help children and the proposals made to undo widespread damage seem so crude that they appear unrelated to the age in which we live. One is forced to realize how small are the islands on which the knowledge of child development is really being put to work. In a project under the O.E.O. anti-poverty program to assist five and a half million elderly citizens, it was announced that 18,200 elderly people would be employed to help neglected and retarded children and the bedridden elderly. One of the first phases of the project, described as "foster grandparents," proposed that the elderly people employed should serve as "substitute parents" for neglected children in institutions. In announcing this program the accompanying statement said:

> At any given moment there are an estimated 21,000 unwanted or neglected babies, toddlers and very young children being held in charity wards, institutions for abandoned children, pediatric and general hospitals. They are exposed largely to efficient, routinized hospital and institutional procedures provided by a generally overworked staff. . . . the program will employ men and women aged 60 and above to help prevent stunting emotional growth in children.[38]

This statement epitomizes the lack of progress in making people aware of the importance of preventing the stunting of the emotional growth of children and of what needs to be done to prevent such stunting. It sometimes seems as though the need to make in-depth mental health service available to the individual poses such vast problems that we will try any panacea that is

[37] *In the matter of Jane Higgins*, 46 Misc.2d 233 (1965).
[38] *New York Times*, August 29, 1965.

offered instead. Recognition of the problem is a first step, and the involvement of government programs is encouraging, but occasional eyedropper doses of tender loving care are not enough.[39] We must move from such goals as the provision of aspirin tablets to consideration of the existence of thousands of children separated from any mothering person with whom they can maintain a meaningful relationship. This goal will require not only the first-aid measure provided by the Office of Economic Opportunity but a determination to end methods of care recognized as destructive to children.[40]

At an American Academy of Pediatrics symposium in 1961, the Children's Bureau of the Department of Health, Education, and Welfare, spurred on by reports of an increase in the number and violence of parental attacks on infants and young children, assembled information and started action. It had previously developed a legislative guide to assure identification, protection, and treatment for such children.[41]

In a 1963 pamphlet the Bureau insisted that cases of injury inflicted by parents "must be promptly called to the attention of appropriate agencies of government for investigation and such action as reasonably may be indicated, whether these cases are referred to social welfare agencies or the courts."[42] The pro-

[39] "The infant's biological needs for the care-taking adult's constant presence is disregarded in our Western culture, and children are exposed to long hours of solitude owing to the misconception that it is healthy for the young to sleep, rest and later play alone. Such neglect of natural needs creates the first breaks in the smooth functioning of the processes of need and drive fulfillment" (Anna Freud, *Normality and Pathology in Childhood*, p. 156).

[40] "That severe disturbances of socialization arise when *identification* with the parents is *disrupted* through separations, rejections, and other interference with the emotional tie to them has been emphasized first by August Aichorn (1925), abundantly proved by John Bowlby (1944) and has been generally accepted as established fact" (*ibid.*, p. 179).

[41] U.S., Department of Health, Education, and Welfare, Children's Bureau, *Proposals for Drafting Principles and Suggested Language for Legislation on Public Welfare and Youth Services* (Washington, D.C.: Government Printing Office, 1957).

[42] U.S., Department of Health, Education, and Welfare, Children's Bureau, *The Abused Child, Principles and Suggested Language for Legislation on Reporting of the Physically Abused Child* (Washington, D.C.: Government Printing Office, 1963).

posed legislation required that when a physician had reasonable cause to suspect that physical injury had been inflicted by a parent or person responsible for the care of a child, neither he nor the institution should have any discretion in the matter of notifying the appropriate policy authority. "Reasonable cause" was defined as (1) the absence of any reasonable possibility that the injury was accidental; (2) infliction of injuries within the family setting; or (3) the physician's judgment, based on his professional experience.

The proposed legislation seemed to assume the existence of adequate, workable social machinery for the protection of children and for dealing with the persons responsible once the notification of "reasonable cause" had been made. It required immediate investigation by the police or the public welfare agency. It further assumed that the matter would be brought before the juvenile court, and that the adults involved might possibly be subject to the jurisdiction of the criminal courts. Since 1963 the Children's Bureau has actively promoted state legislation to require physicians to report cases where there is evidence that a child's injuries might have been inflicted by his parents or persons having custody of him. In 1960 only one state, California, had legislation to protect children from physical abuse. By August, 1965, Mrs. Oettinger, Chief of the Children's Bureau, announced that forty-six states had adopted such laws.[43] In making

---

[43] Twenty-five states acted in 1965 (Children's Bureau Release, August 26, 1965). Only Alabama, Hawaii, Mississippi, Virginia, and the District of Columbia had failed to enact abuse statutes. However, the legislation varies from state to state. The State of Illinois Department of Children and Family Services issued regulations requiring all physicians who had reason to believe that an injury sustained by a child under sixteen was due to physical abuse or neglect to make an immediate report to the Department. Such reports might also be made to the local law enforcement agency, with notice to the Department. The Department, on such notification, was required to make an immediate investigation and provide directly or through a voluntary agency protective services to prevent further abuse. It was also required to file a petition in the appropriate court to seek removal of the child when it was deemed necessary (Illinois, Children and Family Service Regulation, No. 2, 42, June 1, 1965).

In Colorado, where there is cause to believe that injuries of a child are not due to accident, reporting by a physician to the proper law enforcement agency has been made mandatory. "Law enforcement agency" is defined to mean the police department in incorporated municipalities and the office of the sheriff in unincorporated areas. In turn, the law enforcement agency is required to submit such reports to the Colorado State Department of Public Welfare, which

this announcement, Mrs. Oettinger stated that she saw the legislation as a necessary step but only as a beginning in getting at the problem. While admitting that there was no exact knowledge as to how many "battered babies" there were in the United States, she stated that "we do know the number is growing." Mrs. Oettinger noted that the cases were "not limited to any one segment of our population—either by level of income or occupation" and emphasized the importance of providing protective services and substitute homes where necessary to protect a child from further and serious injury:

> It is likely that it [physical abuse of children] will be found to be a more frequent cause of death than such well recognized and thoroughly studied diseases as leukemia, cystic fibrosis and muscular dystrophy, and may well rank with automobile accidents and the toxic and infectious encephalites as causes of acquired disturbances of the central nervous system.[44]

A subsequent study by a group of workers in the Massachusetts Society for the Prevention of Cruelty to Children reported growing evidence from various areas of the country of physical abuse by parents, repeated injuries, and instances of resultant deaths. This report sought to gather and analyze data on 134 cases involving about 200 children who were reported to have been abused in one year.[45] In 86 per cent of these cases the abuse was committed by either the mother or the father. The parents were found to have many problems and to be relatively young. Three distinct clusters of personality characteristics were identi-

---

is charged with investigation, the provision of protective services, and the institution of court action where indicated (Colorado, *Revised Statutes,* [1963] c. 22, Art. 13).

In 1963 Pennsylvania enacted a law making it mandatory on physicians, interns, residents, hospitals, and pharmacies to report on "injuries by deadly weapon or criminal act." Under the Pennsylvania act adults are to be reported to the chief of police and children under eighteen to the presiding judge of the juvenile court or to the community child protective agency, where such court or service exists. In their absence, reporting is to be made to the police (Act 492 of August 24, 1963, Amending Act of June 24, 1939, Commonwealth of Pennsylvania).

[44] Editorial, "The Battered Child Syndrome," *Journal of the American Medical Association,* CLXXXI, No. 1 (July, 1962), 42.

[45] Harold D. Bryant *et al.,* "Physical Abuse of Children," *Child Welfare,* XLII, No. 3 (March, 1963), 125–30.

fied: hostility and aggressiveness traceable to early childhood experience; rigidity, compulsiveness, and lack of warmth; and strong feelings of passivity and dependence, so that parents competed with their children for the love and attention of their spouses. In this group general depression was frequently interwoven into the personality pattern; a significant degree of physical disability among fathers, many of whom were dependent on wives for support, was also noted. It was found that in general one child in the family was selected for abuse and that, once begun, there was a tendency for the abuse to be repeated against the selected child.

In decisions concerning treatment three factors appear of primary importance: the degree and extent of pathology in the family, the apparent need of immediate protection for the child, and the prognosis for success in helping the parent to effect change. In reviewing the literature the investigators found an unfortunate separation of the medical, psychiatric, and legal aspects of these problems. They recognized the importance of continuing social work with the families but found that even when the "battered baby" was identified, community responsibility for dealing with the problems was undefined. They saw the need for a more comprehensive approach, which would include protection of the child and social treatment of the family.

In another study legislation without thoughtful implementation that would include adequate diagnostic and casework treatment services was viewed as unsound:

> Even gross criteria must be developed to differentiate the parents who can utilize professional help from those whose personality development has been so arrested, twisted, warped and fixed that the most highly skilled professional staff cannot now help them develop into adequate parents. . . . Someone must bear the responsibility for identifying and acting on behalf of the child whose right to health conflicts seriously with the rights of parents who cannot be helped to meet their responsibilities before the child sustains physical or emotional injury.[46]

[46] Helen E. Boardman, "Who Insures the Child's Right to Health?" *Child Welfare* (July, 1963), p. 7. Mrs. Boardman had previously presented a series of 12 parents believed to have inflicted trauma; six of the children were under

While accurate histories are seldom obtainable, the development of radiology has given additional support to the judgment of the experienced clinician who suspects deliberate injury to an infant or young child. Dr. Lawrence Finberg, Chief of the Division of Pediatrics at Montefiore Hospital in the Bronx, reports that while the history given is usually that the baby either fell from a bed or chair or that an arm or leg became caught in the slat of a crib, "when something was found on X-ray, such as fracture, the odds have been four out of five (80%) that the trauma was deliberate and not accidental."[47] Despite the development of such objective methods of identification, medicine, law and social agencies have all been slow and ineffective in preventing or controlling child abuse.

In discussing the medical implications of physical abuse of children, Dr. Philip Dodge saw the "battered child syndrome" as a largely unrecognized medical, social, and public health problem. He referred to a study in Massachusetts that showed that although 30 per cent of such children had previously been seen by physicians, only 9 per cent had been referred to protective services for investigation. He believed the basic reason for such inaction to be "the lack of awareness on the part of doctors that adults, particularly parents, may seriously injure and even kill their children."[48] Dodge also found that doctors wished to avoid "legal entanglements" and that many rationalized their

---

12 months and all were under 3½ years of age. All but one had a history of repeated injuries. Three were dead. Two of them had died of injuries that occurred after the parent had been convicted and placed on probation. . .
This indicates the high degree of wishful thinking by courts and protective services and of the danger of assuming such parents have learned their lesson or should automatically be given "another chance." Quoted in Marion C. Morris and Robert W. Gould, "Role Reversal: A Concept in Dealing with the Neglected, Battered Child Syndrome," *Child Welfare* (July, 1963), p. 33.

[47] See Lawrence Finberg, M.D., "A Pediatrician's View of the Abused Child," *Child Welfare* (January, 1965). See also Dr. Richard Galdston, "Observations on Children Who Have Been Physically Abused and Their Parents," *American Journal of Psychiatry*, CXXII, No. 4 (October, 1965), 440–43.

[48] "Medical Implications of Physical Abuse of Children," Paper Presented at the American Humane Association, Children's Division, Symposium on Protecting the Battered Child, National Conference on Social Welfare, 1962. See also Helen E. Boardman, "A Project To Rescue Children from Inflicted Injuries," *Social Work*, VI, No. 1 (January, 1962), 43–51.

failure to act on the grounds that 50 per cent of such children were likely to suffer repeated injuries.

Such an approach to child abuse by physicians is hard to comprehend in view of the findings of psychiatrists about the personalities of the parents involved and the physical danger to their children. Dr. Irving Kaufman expressed the view that unless interrupted or modified, child abuse by a parent, like other types of pathology, becomes incorporated into the parent's behavior. While supporting efforts to help parents to deal with their emotional problems, Dr. Kaufman warned of many situations in which the parent's pathology is so severe, deep-seated, and dangerous to the life and health of the child that his removal from the home may be necessary.[49] In regard to the long-range effects of child abuse, he referred to a study of childhood schizophrenia in which it was reported that "the anti-social type of schizophrenic tended to come from this type of disruptive home with such violently abusive parents who demonstrated uncontrolled aggressive and sexual behavior, and who were unrelated to the community."[50]

Dr. Kaufman found that parents who engage in child abuse often are people who work, keep house, and do relatively well in many areas of living but who under stress may be subject to outbursts of violence, delusional thinking, and disturbed behavior. Commitment to a psychiatric hospital leads to discharge as soon as a remission is reported. In view of this description, it is small wonder that the future threat to the welfare of a child presented by such parents is difficult for the courts to evaluate. As noted by Dr. Kaufman, these parents, like ambulatory schizophrenics, show little overt evidence of psychosis although close observation may reveal psychotic patterns in their thought processes. In addition, judges are often incredulous when faced with allegations that a parent has battered his own infant. The lack of evidence of previous wrongdoing or of injury to other children in

[49] "Psychiatric Implications of Physical Abuse of Children," Paper Presented at the American Humane Association, Children's Division, Symposium on Protecting the Battered Child, National Conference on Social Welfare, 1962.

[50] "Four Types of Defense in Mothers and Fathers of Schizophrenic Children," *American Journal of Orthopsychiatry*, XXXIX, No. 3 (July, 1959), 460–72.

the family, the reasonably adequate adjustment in other areas of life, and the persistent assertions of innocence by the parents make the charges all but incomprehensible to the judge. They run counter to his personal experience. As one judge said, after hearing expert testimony, based on radiological evidence, that a series of bones had been broken in an infant, "I just can't believe a mother would willfully hurt her own child." Even when there is competent evidence by a radiologist that the injuries found through X-rays are not consistent with the history of injury given by the parents, judges may not regard such evidence as sufficient to warrant a finding of neglect against a specific parent.

In the absence of any apparent mental illness, the court has no power to order a psychiatric study of the parent unless it first makes a finding of neglect. The problem for the court is made still more difficult when a petition is filed by a social agency, hospital, or public welfare department that does not submit adequate evidence. With little awareness of the requirements of due process, or the necessity of excluding hearsay reports, the agencies are frustrated when the court finds it must dismiss such a petition. The judge, in turn, may realize that because the infant involved cannot defend itself, he may be dooming it to further abuse.[51] Certainly no warning lecture can be expected to provide protection for the child against a future outburst of violence by the parent in a situation of stress.

That abuse of children will continue regardless of legislation is as certain as that other crimes will continue. However, further study and the sharing with doctors, social agencies, and those who shape and enforce our laws of what is learned by psychiatrists is essential. The courts before which such cases appear will need skillful advice as to when the parents can be helped without removal of the child and when removal is the only possible protection against further serious damage to the child.

[51] See *In the matter of S.*, 46 Misc.2d. 161 (1965). Judge Harold Felix held that the condition of the infant spoke for itself and permitted a finding of neglect when an infant suffers serious injuries in his home for which there is no satisfactory explanation. See also Monrad G. Paulsen, "The Legal Framework for Child Protection," *Columbia Law Review*, LXVI, No. 4 (April, 1966), 678–717.

In one case in New York City a five-week-old infant was taken by her mother to a hospital, where severe lacerations of the vagina and bleeding from the mouth were found. It was learned that two years earlier the mother had brought her three-week-old son to the hospital because of bleeding from the mouth. At that time an X-ray had shown a skull fracture and a suspicious mouth lesion for which there was "no clear explanation." No action had been taken by the hospital to protect the infant, and he had been discharged to the parents. Twelve days later he had been returned to the emergency room and had been found dead on arrival. *Post mortem* examination had revealed two skull fractures, fractures of three ribs, and internal hemorrhages. When interviewed by the Chief Medical Examiner of New York County one day after the death of the infant, the father had admitted "dropping" the baby. In the opinion of the Medical Examiner, this explanation could not account for the old and new injuries found during the autopsy, but no legal action had been taken. When the findings on the second infant were reported, the New York City Department of Welfare filed a petition through its protective services. At the preliminary hearing the court ordered psychiatric observation of both parents. The father was found insane and committed to a state hospital. Only after commitment had occurred did the mother dare to speak of her nightmarish life with her husband, of her fear of him, and of his abuse of her and of the infants. She had entered the marriage against the wishes of her parents, who regarded the husband as inferior. The mother was better educated than he, had come from a family of superior culture, and believed that if she stood by her husband, he would change. She did not wish to admit failure and also feared her husband. With the help of her family, and freed from fear of her husband, she was able to accept psychiatric help and become a good mother to the surviving child.

In 1964 the juvenile courts in this country are reported to have handled 686,000 juvenile delinquency cases excluding traffic offenses. Of these cases 26.8 per cent involved such conduct as truancy, ungovernability, and running away, all of which are only violations of the law when committed by children. The vast majority of the offenses were committed against property, and only 9 per cent involved offenses against a person such as homicide, assault, and rape or other sex offenses. Over half of these cases were handled non-judicially, without the filing of a formal petition. (Most juvenile courts now have "intake departments" where approximately half of the cases referred to the courts are "adjusted" on an informal basis.) Analysis of court dispositions showed that 30 per cent of the juveniles were dismissed, 50 per cent were placed on probation, and 20 per cent were committed to the care and custody of an agency or institution.[52]

In addition to the large number of children handled by the juvenile courts, there is a high proportion of children taken into custody by the police who never are referred to court. A few studies suggest that the police often rely on improper criteria in determining who shall and who shall not be referred for court action: "One study concluded that the determinative factors are the juvenile's demeanor, his appearance and his race; another confirms the reliance on race and notes wryly that 'athletes and altar boys will rarely be referred to court for their offenses.' "[53] Similar criticism has been directed at the criteria for case "adjustment" by court intake departments.

To what extent delinquent children have been benefited by the juvenile courts over the past sixty-five years is unanswerable. While the cruelty and injurious effects of jail and prison confinement have been largely eliminated since the establishment of such courts, the reformatories and state training schools that replaced the prisons were for years but little less harsh and destructive.[54] In some places there were efforts to provide care, education, and treatment and to fulfill the purposes of the legislation, but only a small minority of the children placed by the courts

[52] U.S., Department of Health, Education, and Welfare, Children's Bureau, *Juvenile Court Statistics, 1964* (Children's Bureau Statistical Series, No. 83; Washington, D.C.: Government Printing Office, 1965).

[53] David R. Barrett, William J. T. Brown, and John M. Cramer, "Juvenile Delinquents: The Police, State Courts and Individualized Justice," *Harvard Law Review*, LXXIX, No. 4 (February, 1966), 782.

[54] See Albert Deutsch, *The Mentally Ill in America.*

were thus provided for. Repeated attempts of children under criminal court age to pretend that they were older reflected not only their hope that they could more easily "beat the rap" in the criminal courts, where procedural requirements were strict, but also reflected their preference for "doing time" for a short period over indefinite confinement under the juvenile court laws.[55]

While papers, conferences, and seemingly endless volumes reiterate the need to work with the child or youth in his family and to change the conditions in the family and the community which contributed to his problems, training schools continue to be built remote from family and community. A homeopathic dose of therapy is thrown into a largely custodial program, with agricultural training provided to "rehabilitate" the urban boy, who will return to his urban world in a comparatively short time.

For years in our large cities the juvenile court has been confronted with the problems of adolescent boys of good intelligence but with emotional and social problems that prevented them from using their abilities. In the absence of opportunities for different living arrangements or the therapy they need, the court repeatedly has had to look at psychiatric reports and return the boy to the community for "one more chance," with the knowledge that it was no chance at all; the alternative has been placement of the adolescent in a training school where neither the academic opportunities nor the treatment needed is available.

William, aged 15, the son of a Negro mother and a white father, was such a boy. Tall, appealing, and gentle-mannered, with above average intelligence and a performance I.Q. of 122, he was reading at only the 3.8 grade level. He had been staying out late at night, had been a truant, and had driven with older boys in cars they had stolen. The product of a broken home, too closely attached to his mother, he had been associating only with older boys in an attempt to grow up and find independence. He was described as insecure and bewildered as to

---

[55] "As prison life becomes less restrictive and sentences are shortened, the practical situation may often make the prison disposition more palatable to the inmate than the indeterminate and indecisive disposition of hospitalization" (Jay Campbell, "A Strict Accountability Approach to Criminal Responsibility," *Federal Probation*, XXIX, No. 4 [December, 1965], 35).

where he belonged within the community. The examining psychiatrist stated that continued help, ongoing psychotherapy, and remedial teaching "over a long period of time within or outside of an institution would go far in ensuring a good adjustment eventually for this child." This is the kind of assistance the courts can rarely secure for such a child.

Awareness of what therapy might achieve has given the judge little more than the vexation of knowing that the medicine needed is generally not within the reach of the courts. The existence of a medical diagnosis does not imply that its recommendations can be followed: the judge must act although his action violates the medical prescription. Thus too often the medical advice has only added to the judge's feelings that his decision is a cover-up for the court's failure to provide what is indicated. Unable to share his disquietude with child or parents, the air of certainty which he adopts in an attempt to convey the belief that his decision is "best for the child," like a boomerang, not only hits the child but rebounds upon him.

Edwin was a fifteen-year-old boy who, with a friend, was found to have forced another fourteen-year-old boy to submit to pederasty when he failed to produce the money that Edwin and his friend demanded. Edwin was born out of wedlock and had never known his father. The mother's marriage to an alcoholic terminated in a separation without financial support from the husband. She worked long hours and was unable to provide adequate supervision. A current boy friend of the mother's spent some nights at the home. The mother, an unskilled worker, had completed only the fourth grade. Edwin had lived with a maternal grandmother until he was eleven. He had done well in school, and his mother expressed interest and pride in his progress. After school he spent most of his time looking at television at home. His mother expressed shock at his behavior and asked for help but hoped he might remain at home.

The court referred the boy for psychiatric evaluation. The psychological report showed that although his fund of information was limited, he was within the average range in intelligence and was superior in comprehension and in capacity for abstract thinking. Results of his projective tests were interpreted as portraying severe disturbance, preoccupation with sexuality, castration fears, and hostile feelings against his mother. Self-destructive tendencies were noted. The psychiatric examiner described him as a pleasant-looking, shy, and ingratiating teenager whose motivation for improvement was "currently high." On the basis of a collateral interview the mother was described as overcontrolling and too ambitious for her son. She was described as "totally lacking in insight, but interested in her son's welfare and reliable." The concluding recommendation of the clinic psychiatrist was that, if probation was to be considered, "then it is imperative that this youth be placed in the hands of a competent male psychiatrist." Remedial reading and casework to keep close track of the boy's progress, to give the mother insight, and to curb her over-control of the boy's activities were also recommended. None of these services were available to the court, and all these recommendations were therefore totally unrealistic. It is doubtful whether the clinic psychiatrist had any knowledge of such resources or felt any obligation to look for them. The prescription could not be filled.

No intensive or widespread effort is as yet being made to provide services for the child and his family where he lives. Instead, despite all the fine talk about looking at the whole child, a first offense is likely to mean probation. Probation too often means one required visit to the home by a probation officer, who sees one parent, as though the other did not exist, followed by regular or occasional reporting to a probation officer. The probation officer, who is usually without professional training and over-whelmed by cases, whose fat bulging files he has often inherited and never found time to read, goes through the gestures of probation. The understanding help of a skilled adult who might break down the child's skepticism and suspicion, created by a hostile world, is not available. Probation fails, and the child who has not changed—who is living in the same home, in the same community, subject to the same destructive pressures—is then categorized a recidivist and sent away, generally to a state training school.

Mental health knowledge and practical experience have demonstrated the need for smaller institutions and expanded services for delinquent children. Yet the creation of smaller institutions, treatment services, and adequate work with the child on his return to the community and with the family before his return, have moved slowly.

On June 30, 1963, there were 38,500 children living in public training schools for delinquent children, at an estimated cost for the fiscal year of $125 million.[56] Of the children admitted or returned during the year, 26 per cent were recidivists. Despite evidence that the rate of recidivism increases when the institution has a capacity of more than 150 children, as shown in the table below,[57] 44 per cent of the public training schools had such capacities.

Median Return Rate, by Size of Institution, 1963

Less than 150 children .... 17.1 per cent
150–299 children .... 28.6 per cent
300 or more children .... 34.4 per cent

The lack of community involvement in what is actually being done for or to children by the juvenile courts in this country under our present laws has led to the denial of adequate services and to cyclical attacks upon the court system. The failure to re-examine the functioning of the courts in the light of modern knowledge has resulted in their being treated alternately as whipping boy and sacred cow. Progress in the mental health field has expanded the focus of interest from the child to his development within his family. However, conceptual thinking and experimental work have remained remote from actual practice in the courts. The judicial fact-finding and disposition of cases has continued to remain largely in the hands of judges untrained in sociology, anthropology, or mental health.

The old-fashioned approach of common sense joined with alternating doses of kindness and sternness (according to the atti-

---

[56] U.S., Department of Health, Education, and Welfare, Children's Bureau, *Statistics on Public Institutions for Delinquent Children*, 1963 (Washington, D.C.: Government Printing Office, 1964). The over-all decrease of the population was about 1 per cent between 1962 and 1963, during which time the population aged ten to seventeen years increased by about 4 per cent (p. 3).

[57] *Ibid.*, p. 5.

tude of the judge and the community climate of the moment) prevails as the accepted stereotype for judicial behavior. With its continuance, the vast increase in the number of cases to be considered simply means that the judge must apply this "commonsense" approach at a faster and faster pace. The results of this mass production are not questioned, criticized, or subjected to any kind of scientific and searching evaluation either within or outside the courts. The authoritarian approach, the preaching at parent or child, is apt to be more satisfying to the judge than helpful to child or parent. The exercise of authority that commands momentary docility can hardly be expected to be lasting or beneficial. On the other hand, there is no significant intervention in the situation by those in the mental health field. Even though some psychiatrists express shock as a result of an accidental encounter with the courts, they are all too likely to turn away to areas where they will not be subject to further shock.

The basic question as to whether in our society a court should continue to dispose of the lives of children is rarely raised. Instead, ivory-tower pronouncements continue to issue from law schools, emphasizing procedural improvements (such as advising children of their rights), changing the language or categories established by law, and the review of cases. In England, where psychiatry is far less generally accepted than in this country, more basic questions have been asked by the government and its advisers. In recent proposals to Parliament, questions about the role of law and of the courts in the lives of children have been discussed. These proposals note that the juvenile courts were created in 1908, and that

> there has been an increasing weight of informed opinion over the last ten years in favor of changes in our methods of dealing with children and young persons under 16 who now come before our courts. . . . We believe that these arrangements should be radically changed because:
>
> 1.   Children should be spared the stigma of criminality.
> 2.   In the great majority of cases . . . before the juvenile courts, the facts are not in dispute. The problem is to decide the appropriate treatment, and the court procedures, designed essentially for testing evidence, do not provide the best means for directing social

inquiries and discussing possibilities with the child's parents and the social services that might be concerned with treatment.

3.   . . . the present arrangements do not provide the best means of getting parents to assume more personal responsibility for their children's behavior.

4.   Discussions as to treatment are made in the form of a court order. This does not allow sufficient flexibility in developing the child's treatment according to his response and changing need.[58]

Having clearly set forth these conclusions, the proposals then move toward creating local family councils consisting of social workers and other persons selected for their understanding and experience with children and adults likely to come before them. These councils would deal with each case as far as possible in consultation with parents, and only where the facts are in dispute would cases be referred to court. Observation centers suitably equipped and staffed to evaluate children would be made available to family councils. If residential care should be required, such observation centers would advise the local authority on the selection of the place best suited to meet the child's needs. Whether these proposals are subsequently implemented or no, their significance lies in their simple and direct questioning of an established institution and approach to new methods consistent with previous experience in the field. The lack of professional jargon to obscure acceptance or understanding is also refreshing.

In approaching this problem the British have an easier mechanism for change than we do, in that the relationship of the national government to the local county or borough is direct and unburdened by constitutional limitations imposed by states' rights. The presentation to Parliament quoted above, therefore, is based not only on the right to seek improvement in the services for children in trouble, but on the acceptance of national responsibility for planning, supervision, and support of the local bodies. One of the most discouraging obstacles to securing adequate services for children in this country continues to lie in the

[58] Great Britain, Secretary of State for the Home Department, *Parliamentary Papers*, Cmnd. 2742, "The Child, the Family and the Young Offender," p. 5.

widely varying attitudes and capacities of the states toward help to children.[59]

To those parents who take the initiative to seek help for emotionally disturbed children, our mental health services and the law must often appear as formidable and bureaucratic institutions from which only the most persistent and lucky are able to secure help. David, a boy of nine, the oldest of six children, was brought to the intake section of a juvenile court by his father, who described his truancy, misbehavior at school, and constant thefts from home and neighbors. A few weeks later the case was marked "adjusted" when the school reported the case had been referred to a school guidance counselor. A year later the father again brought the child to the court intake service to ask help for continuing problems at school and continuing stealing from home. This time the case was marked "adjusted" on referral to a social agency. The father appeared for the third time three months later, stating that the boy was beyond control and that he continued to steal. In answer to a phone call the agency worker reported that the boy seemed seriously disturbed. He was finally referred to the court for a petition by the father alleging incorrigibility, truancy, and stealing. A hearing was held, with a law guardian appointed to represent the child, and a finding was made against the child. The child was remanded to a detention home for a month pending a psychiatric study.

[59] The simplest example is to be found in our laws, under which the federal government reimburses the states on a matching basis for aid given to children where there is no father in the home. The aid has been kept at a level in all states far too low to bring aid for these children even up to the poverty line. However, the amount of aid varies from less than thirty cents a day to a little over one dollar a day. Again, although the federal government has amended its program for aid where the father is in the home but unable to support the family, only a minority of the states have taken advantage of it. The result is that in the majority of states in order to assure support for a wife and children through Aid to Dependent Children, the father must disappear or seem to disappear. Professor James E. Starrs writes that "like other legal processes in the South, the juvenile courts may be no more than another strong arm of segregation." He also quotes from the 1965 report of the U.S. Commission on Civil Rights, which found that southern juvenile courts utilize "the latitude permitted in juvenile proceedings to curtail or penalize participation in constitutionally protected rights" ("Southern Juvenile Courts—A Study of Irony, Civil Rights and Judicial Practice," *Crime and Delinquency*, XIII, No. 2 [April, 1967], 291).

When interviewed by a probation official the mother reported her efforts to get help for this child not only through visits to the intake of the court, the school guidance counselor, and the social agency, but by taking him directly to a hospital, where she was told that there were no openings. Both parents expressed concern not only for the boy's stealing but because at times they seemed unable to reach him. He had suffered from asthma until he was three and had been enuretic since that age. When interviewed, the child asked for placement, saying he did not like his parents, but then added quickly that he knew they liked him or they would not have brought him to court to get help. The child appeared intelligent but depressed; when asked what he would like to be, he stated: "I don't want to be nothing." In speaking to the social agency to whom this family had been referred earlier, the probation officer was told that at the intake interview the boy had appeared quite disturbed but that the agency could not see the family for further work-up because it was unable "to give any service until the fall." When the psychiatric study was finally completed and the case came back to the court, nineteen months had elapsed from the date on which these parents first sought help. Referrals had drawn blanks, the psychiatric study was delayed, and all the machinery of the law had to be invoked in an adversary proceeding between a father and a ten-year-old child in order to secure clinical advice on his need for residential care.

Chapter V

THE WAR AGAINST POVERTY, THE ROLE
OF LAW, AND MENTAL HEALTH

L aw and psychiatry are both in their infancy as far as services to the poor are concerned. Both are restricted by the swaddling clothes of tradition, which have prevented them from reaching out to provide meaningful services to the poor, except in limited fashion. Neither is prepared to assume the broad and deep responsibilities to the poor that have become part of a new ideal for American society.

While the traditional teachings of law have required equal justice and the traditional teachings of medicine have required service to all who need it, these teachings have too often been honored in the breach rather than in the observance, so far as the poor are concerned. The impact of law and psychiatry has been so vastly different in the lives of those who can and those who cannot purchase skilled services that no statistics with average or median figures can reflect it. Equality before the law or in mental health services has not been made a meaningful right to the poor. For long periods of human history poverty, like mental illness, was regarded first as the will of God and then as an incurable condition. The concept that those conditions can be corrected by social and medical institutions, if given the proper tools and the people to employ them, is comparatively modern.

The search for social institutions in our society that may help to cure or correct the individual tragedies resulting from poverty and to prevent its continuation or recurrence in the lives of many people is a new approach. As in the development of new medical or health measures to control or prevent other pestilences, there

is need for research, for trial and error, for the development of
new techniques and new professional personnel. It may well be
necessary to examine to what extent law and the mental health
professions have unwittingly been carriers of the disease of poverty, have helped to perpetuate it, and have prevented recovery
from its debilitating effects. Thus far, neither profession has provided adequate leadership in seeking or securing social change.
Despite daily involvement with the problems of the human beings who come to them professionally, only a small minority of
lawyers and doctors have actively concerned themselves with the
problems of people whose conduct or mental illness have caused
them to be rejected by society as deviants, or who are classifi-
able as "poor."

"Successful" practitioners in the one group for the most part
have served the upper economic group in a one-to-one therapeutic relationship. They have avoided the state hospitals, the courts,
and the problems that are toughest. "Successful" lawyers in the
other group have usually served business clients and have avoided
the task of discovering and asserting the rights of the poor and
troubled.

Until recently only a few men in either field had accepted
responsibility for these new tasks. Today, the necessity of social
change has begun to pose a challenge to both groups. Practitioners in the mental health field have begun to recognize the broader
problems that require their talent—the need for transforming the
custodial, non-therapeutic state hospitals for the mentally ill, the
social problems of troubled families, the importance of the environment in which people live, and the effects of segregation
and rejection on mind and body.

The validity of the psychological tests used in the juvenile
courts has been questioned because they are largely constructed
on the basis of experience with middle-class subjects. According
to two clinical psychologists,[1] the delinquent child from the lower
socioeconomic groups seeks to ward off contact with the examiner, and may respond to projective techniques as childish or

---

[1] Carmi Harari and Jacob Chwast, "Class Bias in Psychodiagnosis of Delinquents," *Crime and Delinquency*, X, No. 2 (April, 1964), 145–51.

demeaning. We are warned of the danger of equating lack of verbal response with lack of intellectual capacity, and the two writers express the belief that the delinquent's productivity during tests may not reflect his performance in a more familiar situation. In a study based on three years of interviewing and observation of twenty-one pre-school children of "multi problem, hard-to-reach families," Dr. Charles Malone has given a vivid description of the disparity between the development of these children and that of children who have not suffered persistent deprivations.[2] Dr. Malone found retarded use of language and a minimal capacity to generalize, distrust and intolerance of closeness, and guarded fearfulness. However, the absence of attributes regarded as "normal" for this age group was balanced by the presence of abilities above what one would expect, including acceptance of responsibilities such as crossing dangerous street intersections, feeding babies at night, and making decisions for parents. Dr. Malone saw these children as the products of a pattern of life in which external dangers and emotional deprivations had been inseparably interwoven. Such studies indicate the degree to which the approach to the problems of the poor will have to be modified if services are to meet their needs.

Lawyers have also been slow to face the effects on men, women, and children of legislative and administrative procedures which violate the rights and self-respect of the poor and reduce them to a state of dependency and hopelessness. Trained to protect the legal rights of clients, they are only beginning to be aware of the legal rights of the poor, which are taking on new proportions. No longer limited to the right of representation in serious criminal cases, such rights now are seen to include the assertion and protection of such elemental rights as the right to vote, the right to privacy, the right to move across state lines, the right to have heat in a tenement, the right to be credited with payments made on property that has been repossessed, and the right to all benefits as determined by law, regardless of race or

[2] Charles A. Malone, M.D., "Safety First, Comments on the Influence of External Dangers in the Lives of Children in Disorganized Families," *American Journal of Orthopsychiatry*, XXXVI, No. 1 (January, 1966), 3–12.

color. Such rights will have to be asserted and protected in many new ways.[3]

How laws affect the personal and human rights of those who have property and those who have none is different in many ways.[4] The Park Avenue apartment and the Harlem slum both provide living spaces. One is spacious and luxurious, the other overcrowded and miserable. The occupants of both are human beings; it is the way of life that is different.[5] So long as the problems of survival are worlds apart, perception of the importance of a man's life to himself and in the eyes of the law will not be the same.

Just as the poll tax served as an effective device to prevent voting by Negroes in the South, the high cost of divorce has been an effective device to prevent the ceremonial, legal termination of marriages for the poor. Desertion has become known as the poor man's divorce, and the bigamy, adultery, and illegitimacy of offspring that result are then subjected to legal and social sanctions both by courts and welfare administrators. The consequences in terms of mental health are enormous. Lack of awareness of or indifference to the reasons for non-compliance with what are regarded as the moral and legal requirements of family law affects members of minority groups most directly.

Further confusion and conflicts arise as a result of administrative attitudes and rules which are contradictory. A mother with children born out of wedlock may be threatened with the removal of her children and the termination of welfare assistance on the ground that her home is "unsuitable." Or the "man in the home" who has visited her, who may be the father of only one of her children, is required to move in and support the entire household; she is threatened with denial of further assistance if he does not. The conflict between moral attitudes and reduced costs

[3] Norman Dorsen, Elizabeth Wickenden, Marvin E. Frankel, Stephen J. Pollak, and Charles E. Ares, "Poverty and Civil Rights, a Symposium," *New York University Law Review*, XLI, No. 2 (April, 1966), 328–52.

[4] See Jacobus ten Brock, "California's Dual System of Family Law: Its Origin, Development and Present Status. Part III," *Stanford Law Review*, XVII, No. 4 (April, 1965), 614–82.

[5] See Claude Brown, *Manchild in the Promised Land* (New York: Macmillan, 1965).

is a constant factor and operates regardless of the best interests of the children involved. The law as administered, while refusing to recognize common-law husbands, has thus recognized common-law stepfathers.

The interrelationship between poverty and mental health, like the interrelationship between poverty and the law, has begun to be recognized. The familiar statistics of the high incidence of violations of law among the poor and, therefore, among racial minority groups who suffer discrimination, are also found in the statistics of the high incidence of illness, death, and a shorter life span in the same group.[6] Both the legal and the mental health professions have reason for humility in the light of the problems we face and of their unwillingness to provide leadership in facing them. Concerned members of both professions face continuing apathy among colleagues bent on "success" in their professions and continuing prejudice against and dislike for those who most need their services—the deviant, the asocial, the antisocial, the mentally ill, and "the poor."

Such professional attitudes reflect those of the larger community. Questionnaires have shown that the general public regards the mentally ill with either dislike, distrust, or fear. Physicians and nurses are held in higher regard than psychiatric personnel or those who deal with other than physical problems. Similar questionnaires would certainly show a far higher regard for the lawyer who deals with corporate matters and business problems than for the lawyer who represents the criminal and the delinquent or who is concerned with family problems. Like the mentally ill, offenders against the law, whether old or young, arouse little public sympathy and have no way of promoting their own interests. The lack of feeling of responsibility toward these groups on the part of the public is manifested by the failure to provide those services which seem, in the light of our current knowledge, to offer the best hope for restoration to health or for reha-

---

[6] James Tobin, "It Can Be Done! Conquering Poverty in the U.S. by 1976," *New Republic*, June 3, 1967, p. 16: "The chances that a Negro family is poor are about four times the possibility that a white family is poor. Until the 1960's . . . Negroes were just expected, in the nature of things, to be poor by white standards."

bilitation. Only the small minority within both groups that has money can afford either first-class legal or medical help, and generally, where non-public research and treatment services are available, only this small minority will receive them.

In one of the studies prepared for the Joint Commission on Mental Illness and Health, entitled "Community Resources in Mental Health," the authors describe as hopeful the genuine concern they found that action be taken to meet the great problem of mental illness. Yet they also noted the neglect of millions of children with mental health problems and the widespread lack of understanding of how to launch programs to alleviate these problems.

Public assistance was described as "usually inadequate in amount, haphazardly given, and temporary even though the need remained. It was degrading to the dignity of the recipient who was often forced to beg for help, to accept a grocery order that proclaimed him a reliefer and in some cases to be labeled a pauper in public print."[7]

The official medical organizations have been resistant to adequate mental health services for the poor.[8] They also have repeatedly avoided or postponed consideration of controversial proposals to alleviate social injustices due to inadequate care and to provide preventive medical services adequate to protect physical and mental health. As recently as December, 1965, it was reported that the American Medical Association House of Delegates voted to defer action on a report by its Committee on Human Reproduction pending conferences with "other interested groups," including the American Bar Association. The report in question had noted that forty-four states either ban abortion or permit it only to save the mother's life, and had asked only that abortion be allowed when there was "substantial risk" to the physical or mental health of the mother or unborn child, or when pregnancy was the result of "statutory or forcible rape or incest."

---

[7] *Action for Mental Health*, pp. 110–13.

[8] The newly elected president of the American Medical Association, Dr. Milford O. Rouse, was reported to have said in his inaugural address that the medical profession must oppose the concept that health care is a "right rather than a privilege" (*New York Times*, June 26, 1967, p. 13).

A reference committee of five wrapped up the real questions in legal trappings and decided that the problem was essentially one for resolution by each state through action of its own legislature. They thus abdicated their responsibility as physicians and passed on to legislatures composed of laymen an issue involving the physical and mental health of mothers and a judgment of the best interest of the mother and child.

In August, 1964, the American Bar Association presented its annual merit award for outstanding public service and professional activities to the Alabama State Bar Association. The award was given in recognition of the state association's adoption and enforcement of strict disciplinary rules to curtail the granting of "quickie" divorces where residence requirements were not met. In the *New York Law Journal* report of this award, it was stated that "the Alabama Bar is integrated, meaning that all lawyers in the state are required to be members of the state association." This accolade was given in a year marked by violence against citizens asserting their civil rights in Alabama. There was no evidence that the Alabama State Bar Association had recognized any professional or moral obligation to defend or represent such citizens. Marvin Frankel reported that after reading the official publication of the Alabama Bar from 1954 to 1964 he found dozens of articles condemning and defying the United States Supreme Court for its decision in *Brown* v. *Board of Education*, but not a single article dissenting from this position. The date of the Supreme Court decision was described as "Black Monday" in the publication.

> Article after article treated States' Rights, the glorious Confederacy, Negro inferiority, the Supreme Court's communistic, atheistic, nihilistic destruction of the Constitution. . . . Nowhere through the decade was there a single dissenting piece. . . . Year in and year out every issue of this official organ of an integrated bar supplies heady reminders that it is written by white men for white men. . . . Such are the sentiments published in this "official organ" of the entire Alabama bar, supposedly including its nonwhite members.[9]

[9] Marvin E. Frankel, "The Alabama Lawyer 1954–1964. Has the Official Organ Atrophied?," *Columbia Law Review*, LXIV (November, 1964), 1247, 1253, 1254.

In happy contrast, the American Bar Association, at its annual convention in 1965, enacted a resolution supporting the development of legal services for the poor under the aegis of the poverty program. A few months later it joined in a conference under the joint auspices of the Department of Justice and the Office of Economic Opportunity to explore what needed to be done and how the legal rights of the poor could be protected. It was the Office of Economic Opportunity that stimulated the bar to consider the legal rights of the poor and offered public funds for this purpose. The warm response of some leaders has been followed by a period of delay, resistance, and concern on the part of many lawyers lest such a program get out of hand and raise questions that would threaten some of the vested property interests immune from questioning. In some communities associations of the bar or societies for legal assistance to the indigent have seen themselves as the only agencies that should be entrusted with a service to protect the legal rights of the poor. That the poor should be represented in the determination of the policies and procedures of such a program is seen by such associations as a threat to their power and a challenge to their conception of what should be involved in asserting the legal rights of the poor.[10] The assumption that legal assistance to the poor, like other forms of charity, includes the right to give or to withhold the help necessary for them to assert anything more than conventional and limited rights has been prevalent for too long. Like charity, legal aid has distinguished between the "deserving" and "undeserving," as defined by those who have the power to give or deny help. This issue is yet to be resolved.

In a pioneering and provocative article, Edgar and Jean Cahn have expressed concern over the fact that in setting up new programs for the poor the key positions of local policy making and administration are generally given to representatives of society's principal institutions—political, commercial, philanthropic, and educational—who are unaccustomed to criticism, impatience, scrutiny, and even failure to appreciate their efforts. Such men are often at the head of the very institutions that have tolerated

---

[10] Edgar S. Cahn and Jean C. Cahn, "What Price Justice: The Civilian Perspective Revisited," *Notre Dame University Lawyer*, XLI, No. 6 (1966), 927–60.

the conditions now regarded as in need of correction. The Cahns therefore urge the building into war on poverty programs provisions for critical scrutiny, advocacy, and dissent.[11]

As the community faces the problems of the poor, many changes in our laws, in the administration or interpretation of law, and in value judgments will be involved. One of the more obvious examples is the decision of the United States Supreme Court which has finally ruled unconstitutional the Connecticut law that made it a criminal offense for a doctor to prescribe or a clinic to provide contraceptive devices.[12] Here the famous words of Mr. Dooley that the Supreme Court follows the election returns might well be applied. This time, however, the election returns reflected growing concern about the population explosion, increasing fear of that explosion in poor countries, growing acceptance of the fact that children who are wanted have the best likelihood of faring well in life, and awareness of the evidence that the lack of birth control devices adds one more deprivation to the inequities suffered by the poor.

There are still other rights that may prove more difficult to discover, assert, and defend. These can only be made meaningful through the creation of services. Without such services they will remain an illusion and a sham. Let me give two examples:

1. A juvenile court is directed by law to act as a wise parent and provide the help a child needs for his rehabilitation. Study of a specific case reveals a broken and deteriorated home and a child denied both the ordinary decencies of life and emotional support. The diagnostic study reports emotional disturbance and the need for placement in a warm foster home or group home where he can receive therapy. The child is Negro, and there is no such facility. In the absence of the needed service, the court sends the child to a large training school far away, where he will receive no therapy and will be isolated from the world he knows.

2. A baby is born out of wedlock. The mother, a narcotics addict, wishes to surrender her child for adoption. She is told that because she is non-white the child will not be accepted

[11] "The War on Poverty: A Civilian Perspective," *Yale Law Journal,* LXXIII, No. 8 (July, 1964), 1317–52.
[12] *Griswold* v. *Connecticut,* 381 U.S. 479 (1965).

until a specific adoptive home is found. The welfare department refers the child to the sectarian agency of the mother's faith and pays a subsidy for foster-home care. The agency states it has no adoptive homes for non-white children. Despite urging by the court, the welfare department refuses to interfere with the decision of the private agency. It refuses to provide direct services, or to refer across religious lines. The baby grows up as an agency boarder, with no one to press for his right to have a family of his own and to feel that he belongs somewhere.

Administrative agencies disbursing benefits under law have been properly described by Bernice Bernstein as having "power over, but without accountability to, our own beneficiaries."[13] Outside scrutiny and review, as well as constant self-examination, are needed if the rights of the poor are not to be granted or withheld by public and private agencies as though there were no correlative duties on the part of those in power to safeguard and assert the rights of the poor.

Both organized medicine and organized law at this time face the challenge and opportunity for developing within their professions a wide and deep concern for those who require meaningful and constructive services, and both have severe handicaps. They have failed in the past to show adequate concern with such problems. There is a dearth of people who have real knowledge in these sectors of law and medicine. There is a lack of adequate basic or scientific research. There is a lack of sufficient personnel from the fields of psychiatry, psychology, and social work to implement growing programs. There is still a refusal among professional groups to deal with other than one-to-one relationships. There is thus far no large-scale attempt to design new means by which denial of rights and services to the poor can be remedied.

Only slowly, because of new knowledge and pressure from the poor, have we begun to recognize the false rationale for denying services to "the unreachable poor." Concern about families that have lived on welfare for three generations, the rise in delinquency and crime, the increase in illegitimate births, and

---

[13] Bernice L. Bernstein, "Equality of Rights for Public Welfare Clients," Address to the American Public Welfare Association National Biennial Conference, December 3, 1965 (mimeographed).

the higher incidence of alcoholism and narcotics addiction have provided the motivation to extend services to those outside the limited group helped in the past.

The more basic question as to whether public assistance as now given to the poor, with its sub-poverty standards and its humiliating procedures, is consistent with either sound concepts of law or of mental health confronts citizens and members of both professions. The Joint Commission on Mental Illness and Health has written:

> Nor does it appear that our total efforts to relieve or improve conditions in the lower socioeconomic levels are deep and far-reaching, alarmists, who see a Welfare State impending or upon us, to the contrary. We also note the analogy between the state of public services on behalf of the mentally ill, and those for dependent children, broken homes, working mothers, the dependent aged, slum tenants, displaced national groups, deprived minority groups, and the unfortunate or ill-starred in general. Compared to the size of each problem, the social efforts to solve it are impressive in their pretensions but feeble in actuality.[14]

The great naturalist Konrad Lorenz has much to teach us about our care and treatment of those who become mentally ill, emotionally disturbed, or law-breakers. He writes that in the pecking order of the poultry yard, the lower the standing of the individual animal, the more he will be pecked by all and sundry. He also records his observation that after certain animals have been abused and pecked by others, they are doomed unless someone comes to their rescue. The explanation given is that the more pecks and blows received, the more certain it is that escape reactions will be blocked and submissive attitudes will gain control over the victim.[15] Both the legal and the mental health professions face the challenge of alleviating and preventing the blows that have too long been the portion of those least able to withstand them, to encourage escape reactions, and to seek the rescue of those who will otherwise be doomed.

---

[14] *Action for Mental Health*, p. 226.
[15] Konrad Lorenz, *King Solomon's Ring* (New York: Thomas Y. Crowell, 1952), pp. 148, 195.

Chapter VI

NEW LAW FOR THE COMMUNITY
AND COMMUNITY PSYCHIATRY

The various forms of intellectual activity which together make up the culture of an age, move for the most part from different starting points and by unconnected roads. As products of the same generation, they partake indeed of a common character; but of the producers themselves, each group is solitary, gaining what advantages or disadvantages there may be in intellectual isolation. . . . Then come, however, from time to time eras of more favorable conditions, in which the thoughts of men draw more together than is their wont, and the many interests of the intellectual world combine in one complete type of general culture.

Walter Pater, in this description of the Renaissance, has suggested what we are seeking to achieve through uniting law and science to forge a society that will bring opportunity, equality, and hope to more men than any society has ever offered. This country, in reaching out for ways to assure the welfare and free the potential of every man, has committed itself to the creation of a kind of society that has never before existed. There are no blueprints available for achieving this goal. The goal, however, involves an acknowledgment that the welfare of the individual is not based on bread alone, nor on the control of his ideas and emotional life, but on providing opportunities for his development so that he may participate in and enjoy life to the full extent of his ability. Expanding legislative programs to meet the economic, social, and psychological needs of the individual, long submerged and obscured by the pressures of poverty and discrimination, have brought with them a vast enlargement of the

153

role of law. At the same time recognition of the psychological and emotional problems of individuals has greatly expanded the role of the mental health professions.

The need for closing the gaps that prevent joint planning and coordination of effort in these fields is clear.[1] The enactment of legislation in the areas of health, welfare, and education, correction, economic opportunities, and civil rights has made new services necessary. It cannot be hoped that the existing research centers or pioneer programs in mental health have made enough progress to be ready to plan and establish the programs now being mandated by federal, state, and local legislation. Their success will depend on the availability of the services authorized by the new legislation to those whom the legislation is intended to help. However, the establishment of comprehensive community mental health services requires more than legislation to provide funds for the construction of buildings or for salaries. It requires the involvement of such disciplines as psychiatry, psychology, social work, medicine, nursing, political science, and law. It requires experimental projects and broad programs to prevent mental illness, as well as programs to treat those who are ill. If mental health programs are to touch and truly help the "unreachable" poor,[2] those who need such services must be sought out.

For those in the field of mental health, with their limited battalions, such responsibilities raise questions both of the capacity to establish new services and of the best deployment of the trained personnel available. To what extent can the work be done through existing schools, welfare agencies, housing, and other service programs? To what extent will the creative energy

[1] Leonard J. Duhl, M.D., "New Directions in Mental Health Planning," Address at Rutgers University, February 26, 1965 (mimeographed). See also Viola W. Bernard, M.D., "Some Principles of Dynamic Psychiatry in Relation to Poverty," Paper read at the American Psychiatric Association annual meeting, New York City, 1965.

[2] "Among the poor, problems have been met with only a minimal amount of service from the mental health profession. They do get some emergency care. They do get some treatment in clinics. But on the whole, most of our underprivileged citizens who suffer mental illness are in State hospitals" (Duhl, "New Directions in Mental Health Planning," p. 6). See also Nicholas Hobbs, "Mental Health's Third Revolution," *American Journal of Orthopsychiatry,* XXXIV, No. 5 (October, 1964), 822–33.

of new services be bogged down in the framework of established institutions? To what extent will the creation of consultant services for community agencies separate the expert from clinical experience and provide only the appearance of mental health services? With a scarcity of personnel, there is always the temptation to shift people upward to the officer group and then find a dearth of the foot soldiers essential to success in community programs, as in wars.

As mental illness or mental health is understood in relation to the "conditions of life," correcting wrongful conditions through law will become of greater significance to mental health agents in our society. As the conditions of life are shown to contribute to behavior difficulties and mental illness, the legal profession must recognize and appreciate the preventive role of community psychiatry. Only the most naive would expect that legislation alone can develop the structures needed to provide comprehensive mental health programs. Lawyers and psychiatrists together must decide where and how to move. The lawyer's comfortable sense of expertise in drafting legislation for new structures and the psychiatrist's initial discomfort in this area may be transformed as the lawyer begins to see the complex problems involved in implementation and the psychiatrist begins to recognize the value of basing his work on laws that are soundly conceived.

Such mutual appreciation should lead to wider horizons, increasing interchange of ideas, and greater ability to participate in the processes of change. Increased sensitivity to the conditions in which people live will be required. Each profession faces the double task of study in depth on specific problems and relating specialized knowledge to larger problems. In addition to the need for intellectual exploration and creativity, there is a need for administrative talent to coordinate valuable knowledge, experimentation, and service so that they are woven together in a permanent tapestry. "Permanent" here means clearly visible and usable until such time as new discoveries demand modification or replacement.

Extremely difficult times lie ahead for both law and psychiatry. A little hope, like a little freedom, cannot be contained: it must be either smothered or permitted to grow. And like the growth of a human being the development and growth of hope will be uneven. The role of the law in providing the framework within which the individual can grow and the role of psychiatry in providing new insights and encouragement to healthy growth complement each other. Psychiatry is concerned with the treatment of individuals, their restoration to health, and the prevention of mental disorder. The law is concerned with control of antisocial or prohibited conduct, rehabilitation of those who engage in such conduct, and prevention of such conduct. Both fields will inevitably become more concerned with the wellsprings of human behavior as they pursue their goals, and the goals, procedures, research, and personnel in each field must thus become ever more closely interrelated.

If the medical position that when the sense of reality is seriously impaired the individual may be regarded as mentally ill is accepted, psychiatry, like law, must consider what "reality" is for the individual. Pioneers in psychiatry found that their search for knowledge of how to treat and restore health to the mentally ill led them back to those personal experiences which had contributed to maladjustment. In turn, discovery of the relevance of such experiences to mental health led to exploration of the family and social conditions which threatened the individual's sense of worth or hope. The focus had to shift in order to embrace the world that constituted reality for the patient. Just as the organized community, sometimes thought of as government, became concerned with the welfare of more and more of its members, the concept of law had to be expanded to modify and correct the reality situations of an increasing number of people. It became evident that in our complex society fewer and fewer people could be independent in their pursuit of freedom, happiness, or even life itself. Laws that told men what they could or could not do became a more and more insignificant proportion of the totality of law, as it flexed its muscles and sought to meet the challenge of government intervention in a democratic society.

As law and psychiatry, from different positions and vantage points, came to be involved not only more deeply but more widely in the welfare of more people, they found a new kinship of aims and responsibilities. What now may be called the mental health of the community began to involve both professions in joint ventures. In our complex world the freedom of the individual to fulfill his potential to exercise liberty in substance requires active intervention by government through law. In such intervention, the skill and insight which the science of mental health can provide are essential to determine how man can best be enabled to feel free and to function effectively. This is mental health in the broadest sense—neither abstract nor violative of individual freedoms, but truly relevant to the realities of living.

There are many areas in which the law, through statutes, judicial decisions, and administrative agencies (with their broad grants of discretion to the inhabitants of our bureaucracies), exercises extraordinary power over the psychological welfare of individuals. The impact of such power on the recipients of social welfare and their families provides an excellent illustration. The importance of permitting creative, untrammeled experimentation by voluntary agencies and local community groups has been stressed repeatedly by those who oppose federal controls. Little stress and less fervor have been shown in evaluating the effects on individuals of repressive rules, invasion of privacy, and the denial of services or discriminatory treatment.

Psychiatrists may recognize the immediate or long-delayed results of humiliating controls, arbitrary denials of assistance, inadequacy of aid, and oppressive moral sanctions. However, the need for formulating mental health concepts in such a way as to eliminate such factors has not been widely recognized as a responsibility of the mental health profession, any more than the denial of the constitutional rights of the poor has been generally seen as a challenge to the legal profession.

It is reported that in nineteenth-century England an organization known as "The Society for the Abolition of Vice" set as its goal "reforming the morals of persons whose income does not exceed £500 per annum."[3] In recent times, it has been rightly said, "the poor are all too easily regulated." They seem to provide

---

[3] Quoted in Peter Jennson, *Freedom To Read* (Public Affairs Pamphlet No. 344; New York: Public Affairs Press, April, 1963), p. 16.

an ever-present and irresistible dish for hungry moralists. Charles A. Reich has pointed out the attempts to impose by law a moral code on recipients of welfare, who are thus considered a special class—to invade their privacy, to restrict their movements, to require that they take loyalty oaths, and, in short, to interfere with their independence of thought and action as a condition for receiving help. Professor Reich has questioned the constitutional basis for such laws, but he has also pointed out that the invasion of the rights of the poor has gone unchallenged and that "the legal profession does not even know enough about agency practices in the welfare field to be able to identify possible denial of rights."[4] He regards this situation as an indictment of the legal profession and urges that a bill of rights be drawn up for the poor.

It might be said with equal justice that members of the mental health profession also lack awareness of the factors in our society that daily impair the mental health of the poor. There has been far too little acceptance of responsibility either for challenging those conditions and practices which threaten mental health or for setting up standards of care and service geared to preventing mental illness and strengthening mental health.

In view of this lag it is interesting to note that Ernest Jones wrote: "Proceeding on the analogy of his own discoveries through psychopathology, Freud expressed the opinion that the best access to the psychology of the ego might be through investigating the disorders of society." After quoting this passage Dr. Leo Srole points out that despite this professional tradition Freud's perspective is not generally or systematically applied either in clinical practice or in residency training.[5] He gives as a possible explanation the fact that when attention is fixed on a central figure, the background recedes into dimly apprehended and taken-for-granted "surroundings."

It has been suggested that the psychiatrist has a contribution to make to community mental health which is different from that

[4] Charles A. Reich, "Individual Rights and Social Welfare," *Yale Law Journal*, LXXIV, No. 7 (June, 1965), 1245, 1246, 1256.

[5] "Selected Sociological Perspectives," in U.S. Department of Health, Education, and Welfare, *Concepts of Community Psychiatry: A Framework for Training* (U.S. Public Health Service Publication No. 1319; Washington: Government Printing Office, 1965), p. 42.

of the social scientist, lawmaker, or community organizer. This difference is sometimes described as the "focus of the psychiatrist on those issues which lead as quickly as possible toward the prevention or relief of personal suffering." This emphasis is contrasted with that of social scientists and community practitioners, whose priorities are "the development of social theory or the achievement of political and organizational action or general social welfare. . . ."[6] However, examination of the psychiatric services available to relieve personal suffering reveals that they reach only a very small minority of those in need. In contrast, workers in other fields such as teaching, health, welfare, the courts, probation, and parole must face the constant challenge and burden of dealing with the many who suffer. This does not mean that the clinically trained psychiatrist does not have a very special contribution to make. It means, rather, that the knowledge and skills he has need not only to be replicated but translated in terms that can help others to provide relief quickly and skillfully.

Among psychiatrists, as among all other professional groups, there is a division between those who are likely, by reason of temperament, personality, and interests, to be concerned with theory, broad planning, or the individual who needs help and those who are not. There is also a sharp division between those who prefer to study and those who are activists, between those who find it difficult to reach out to other human beings and empathize with their problems and those who are able to do so, between those who are researchers and those who are healers, and perhaps even between those who have an inner dynamo that drives them to help others and those who do not.

There has been a strong difference of opinion among professional workers in the mental health field in regard to the recent surge of interest in broad social issues and involvement in action programs. Opposition has been voiced by those who fear broad social involvement at the expense of the hard day-to-day work that is needed to strengthen the clinical skills and knowl-

[6] Gerald Caplan, M.D., "Current Issues Relating to the Training of Psychiatric Residents in Community Psychiatry," in *ibid.*, p. 173.

edge within the profession. There are also, as in all groups in our society, persons who have little concern for broad social problems and who, by reason of temperament, background, or political viewpoint, resist involvement in the process of social change.

There are other clinicians with an understanding of the effect of social and cultural forces on the mental health or illness of patients, and they have much to contribute to social planning. In the area of prevention, such men have demonstrated that there is cumulative evidence of the relationship between malnutrition and disabilities in learning or functioning which should be presented to legislators. Sometimes they feel that such knowledge is ignored or is not properly presented. Dr. I. N. Berlin has pointed to the lack of expressed concern with the role of the mental health professions in the President's Report and in the Commission Report on Mental Retardation, and also in the choice of emphasis of the Federal Commission on Delinquency. He expresses the viewpoint that such slighting of mental health is due to the failure of professional organizations to take leadership on serious mental health questions involving social issues.[7]

In many ways the conflict of values and the rather belated concern with patients not of the middle class has beset psychiatry as well as law. It is only recently that some medical schools have seriously concerned themselves with introducing those problems and possibilities of service essential to meeting the many mental health needs in our society into the educational curriculum. In commenting on the 1962 conference on psychiatric education, held under the auspices of the American Psychiatric Association, Dr. Fritz Freyhan noted that while there was agreement that the psychiatric program "should be widened toward the primary aim to develop a socially responsible psychiatrist . . . it was also postulated 'that training programs have no obligation to provide personnel for the state hospitals and other public facilities or even to encourage residents to undertake such work.' "[8] In his comments on the conference, Dr. Freyhan said:

[7] Editorial, *American Journal of Orthopsychiatry*, XXXIV, No. 5 (October, 1964), 801, 802.
[8] Dr. Fritz A. Freyhan, "On the Psychopathology of Psychiatric Education," *Comprehensive Psychiatry*, VI, No. 4 (August, 1965), 221–26.

As we are so apt to say about our patients, there is intellectual insight countered by strong emotional resistance. We seem to have drifted into a thoroughly autistic state combining highly idealistic aspirations with a denial of professional obligations and disassociation from social and scientific realities. . . . This culture largely ignores comprehensive therapeutic necessities, limits professional interest to office-treatable patients, and overwhelmingly produces psychiatrists for the more affluent social classes.[9]

Dr. Freyhan pointed to the fact that a large number of training centers have virtually excluded electroshock treatment from their therapeutic programs and have failed to provide psychiatric residents with adequate instruction in the use of drugs or supervision in their administration. He was troubled by the possibility that a negative criterion, "unsuitability for psychotherapy," was being converted into a rationale for drug treatment. With evidence of a strong preference for the non-psychotic middle-class patient of higher education even in training centers, he questioned the scientific basis for the assumption or "rumor that patients of lower economic and educational status respond better to drugs than to psychotherapy."[10] When Dr. Freyhan questioned the educational director of one training center as to what steps were taken to identify and eliminate social bias in selecting patients for psychotherapy, he was told that "it seemed more important that the resident could select a patient with whom he felt comfortable and whom he could like."[11]

Just as study of the law concerning social problems and the courts dealing with them has occupied a lowly place in the scale of values of teachers of law, legal practitioners, and the judicial hierarchy, the efforts of medical schools to develop training activities in community psychiatry have also been so regarded. In a survey of this subject it has been reported that one important factor is psychological:

The resident's interest (and sometimes staff interest as well) is difficult to stimulate and maintain. Residents have a predetermined set toward psychoanalytic type practice and one-to-one psychotherapy. Teaching and supervisory staff often tend to foster this

[9] *Ibid.*, p. 224.
[10] *Ibid.*, p. 225.
[11] *Ibid.*, p. 226.

set. Community mental health activities hold a low place in the psychiatric hierarchy as compared to individual psychotherapy, academic psychiatry, or research.[12]

Happily, more young members of the professions are beginning to question the values that have prevailed. Among them are those who regard the lack of manpower in the helping profession as part of an anti-intellectual trend whose emphasis is on productivity and wealth, while social responsibilities and public service are neglected. There are signs of change in our law schools, where fewer students see acceptance by a big Wall Street firm as the be-all and the end-all of professional achievement. More first-rate students are exploring the opportunities for use of their skills in civil rights, in family law, in work with the poor, and in public administration. So, too, in psychiatric training centers more young people are asking about the meaning of community psychiatry and the possibility of new kinds of service related to the basic conditions which create so many human and social problems. However, in the teaching of law, as in the teaching of medicine, the tradition of preparing the professional student for private practice continues to be dominant, with rare exceptions.[13] Voices have been heard urging modification of the curriculum of law school and psychiatric training, but in both areas there has been stubborn resistance to change.[14]

[12] Robert S. Daniels, M.D., and Philip M. Margolis, M.D., "Community Psychiatry and Training in a Traditional Psychiatric Residency," in U.S. Department of Health, Education, and Welfare, *Concepts of Community Psychiatry*, p. 71n.

[13] Dr. Leo Srole, "Selected Sociological Perspectives," pp. 35, 36. The author states that the notion of viewing "the patient in his social setting, although in many quarters accepted in principle, is too often neglected in practice; witness that except at 'top drawer' medical schools it has thus far only fragmentarily filtered down into clinical procedures and residence training."

[14] Dr. Raymond Feldman, Foreword, U.S. Department of Health, Education, and Welfare, *Concepts of Community Psychiatry*, p. vii: "Perhaps the toughest of the hurdles is the need for the departments of psychiatry, which are responsible for training psychiatrists, to really accept the challenge of providing leadership in community mental health programs." See also Charles A. Reich, "Toward the Humanistic Study of Law," *Yale Law Journal*, LXXIV, No. 7 (June, 1965), 1402, 1403: "Many of the ills of legal education are symptomatic of the fact that it is primarily professional in orientation. . . . Law school education in fact continues to reflect primarily the needs of the profession as the profession is now constituted."

The extension of financial resources to people in need represents the groping of society for ways in which the deprived individual, denied equal opportunities for fulfillment or subject to inner stresses, can be helped. There is a risk that too large a proportion of the new resources may be captured or exploited by small groups within the legal, psychiatric, and social science professions and invested in areas of personal interest, in inflated research projects, or in the buttressing of old institutions in which such groups feel at home and from which they derive power or prestige. The lack of well-trained professionals committed to fulfilling old needs newly discovered and to creating different patterns of education and services is a threat to the effective use of new government resources.

As in the war against poverty, there is real danger that too large a proportion of the aid will be devoured by the middlemen—the transmitting agencies, the bureaucracies hurriedly established or rapidly expanded—and that too little will reach the "poor" for whom it is intended. Existing institutions, long established and well administered, provide attractive conduits for siphoning aid to the recipients. If the discredited theory, put forward in the days of the Hoover depression, that by government investment at the top, wealth or benefits will percolate or trickle downward is revived, the result will be disillusionment, cynicism, and frustration on the part of the many people deprived of the help they have been led to expect. It is easy to muster opposition to new projects when people less well trained, less sophisticated, and unused to being part of the old power structures make errors through "doing." It is far more difficult to discover and correct the more far-reaching errors of old institutions whose "non-doing" constitutes a continuing denial to individuals in need of service.

Despite growing recognition of the role of law in assuring people freedom from want and freedom of opportunity, practitioners devoted to fulfilling the legal obligations created by this recognition are limited in number. This statement is equally true of the psychiatric community, to many of whose members the tradition of treatment for the individual of means remains all but exclusive.[15] Unfortunately, despite professional and even monetary opportunities in new fields of service, status distinctions between those who minister to the "haves" and to the "have-nots" continue to be important.

The need for public facilities to prevent mental illness, to treat the mentally ill, and to provide conditions that will strengthen mental health in the community presents a challenge and also a mandate to those who would administer these resources. One must question whether that mandate can be honorably met if psychiatrists remain within their own institutions, ready to use their skills only for a slowly increasing but still highly selective group of the traditionally "treatable." Happily, a growing number of influential psychiatrists have accepted responsibility that goes beyond the individual accepted for treatment in the private office, the clinic, or the hospital. It is these men who are reaching out to the community and exploring its problems with a view to providing broader service and who are developing community plans and structures based on mental health concepts.[16]

Fulfillment of our society's demand for what has been called a "widening of focus" requires more than the traditional learning and expertise in both law and psychiatry. New insights as to unrecognized needs and rights in our society, new concepts, and new methods of practice must develop. Unhealthy conditions of life must be recognized; rights long neglected must be asserted; the possibility of changes in patterns of relationships must be anticipated.

It has been suggested that the psychiatrist who concerns himself with community psychiatry can choose the most favorable and opportune moments for intervention and make full use of members of other helping professions so that his time will be used most effectively and he will not be overwhelmed by the

---

[15] See Duhl, "New Directions in Mental Health Planning," p. 30: "In one major training center 90 per cent of the staff commented that their training center should be concerned with community psychiatry. Only 10 per cent, however, were willing to participate."

[16] Gerald Caplan, M.D., "Community Psychiatry, Introduction and Overview," in U.S. Department of Health, Education, and Welfare, *Concepts of Community Psychiatry*, p. 5: "The only legitimate limitation of the population focus of the community psychiatrist is the boundary of the community."

task before him.[17] It is questionable whether such a well-regulated existence is possible for anyone who attempts to meet the urgent necessities that confront psychiatry and law at the present time. While there may be those who, either by temperament, by the use of self-protective devices, or by their remoteness from the needs that are not being met, can function without strain, these new responsibilities so directly involve the hopes of countless thousands that the majority of those engaged in community law or in community psychiatry will have no time to slumber for many years to come.

The notion that the community psychiatrist or the lawyer concerned with the discovery and assertion of the rights of the poor can become a general in the rear after developing a chain of command, that he can feel confident that the work will be done adequately by individuals in the field with less and less training, may be attractive but is surely illusory. Such a structure, while safeguarding the personal well-being of the generals, is all too likely to result in avoidance of the direct and challenging experience which should modify concepts and methods. It will leave those who most need services in the hands of those least experienced. It will deprive the community of the highest type of experimentation and exploration of new methods and will reinforce the long-standing separation of first-rate talent and experience from those who most need them. One cannot expect every professor, scholar, physician, or lawyer to engage in community planning or action. Yet the new challenge requires that the creative person should, like the artist or musician, continue to work in the medium that is his, if great masters as well as good artisans and craftsmen are to be developed.[18]

Recognition of the need to have some theoretical framework for understanding the community in which patient or client draws his breath, struggles, and faces life may be a long step forward. However, while exploration of new models is needed, it is

---

[17] *Ibid.*, p. 8.

[18] See Caplan, "Current Issues Relating to the Training of Psychiatric Residents in Community Psychiatry," p. 173: "it follows that the community psychiatrist who does not maintain a close identification with and competence in clinical work loses his capacity to make a specific contribution."

clear that far more intensive first-hand experience with those problems of individuals which have remained below the surface of our concern is required—action in the field to enrich understanding—so that the models constructed will be truly relevant to the task in hand.[19] One cannot expect physicians and lawyers to become experts in the problems of education, housing, employment, health, and discrimination. However, basic breakthroughs cannot be expected if the leadership in these professions is satisfied with a mere smattering of superficial information about the conditions that are contributing to social and personal pathology.

The community psychiatrist and the community lawyer will have many roles to play in terms of direct service, clarification of problems, development of new concepts, adaptation of old procedures, stimulation of new programs, and interpretation of both experience and ideas to the larger community. In these areas specialization is already developing. At this time it would seem that the vast disproportion between the islands of service and the sea of unmet needs requires unusually intensive study before rigid models are created into which those needs are to be fitted— new Procrustean models must be avoided as far as possible, just as the old Procrustean models must be discarded. The lawyer will need to remedy what are now seen, in far broader terms than they once were, as deprivations of rights. The community psychiatrist will have to see that aid is given to more persons in "their active struggle with the realities of their life situation."[20] Both will need to bring to the public attention existing situations that are injurious to individual and community well-being.

---

[19] Leonard J. Duhl, M.D., "The Psychiatric Revolution," in U.S. Department of Health, Education, and Welfare, *Concepts of Community Psychiatry*, p. 24: "The problem of treatment demands an understanding of the relationship of disease to the individual host and to the broader environment in such a way as to know the best place to intervene or what combination of measures are required."

[20] Viola W. Bernard, M.D., "Some Principles of Dynamic Psychiatry in Relation to Poverty," p. 254: "There is . . . need to correct the morally, socially, and psychologically intolerable overconcentration of our resources of highly trained manpower and specialized facilities for the benefit of a generally advantaged minority."

Neither law nor psychiatry must be diverted from recognizing the importance of the needs of the individual. Lawyers and psychiatrists must not let themselves be used to make what is injurious or unjust acceptable to the individual or to the community. The position that "the community goal demands the smallest possible intervention in each instance, consonant with getting the sufferer back onto the track of adjustment and adaptation in the world of reality"[21] may lead to a far too restricted and dangerously unsound goal if used to make an unhealthy *status quo* more tolerable. One must also question whether there is not a danger of imposing new ways of achieving conformity or adjustment to a reality which in itself may be unhealthy and to which maladjustment may be a far more healthy response. Here assumptions that middle-class values have inherent moral or cultural superiority require most careful scrutiny if community health services are not to be misused.[22]

The judgment that what is regarded as primary prevention of mental disorder is more economical than remedial efforts raises questions for the here and now as well as for the role of community psychiatry. While some writers in the field have approved this choice and drawn an analogy to public health services, the development of the public health profession has supplemented but never replaced the expansion of medical service to the individual—quite the contrary.[23] In the field of community psychia-

[21] Caplan, "Current Issues Relating to the Training of Psychiatric Residents in Community Psychiatry," p. 14.

[22] See Dr. Catherine S. Chilman, *Growing Up Poor* (Washington, D.C.: U.S. Department of Health, Education, and Welfare, 1966). Dr. Chilman suggests that in the light of the conformity and materialism prevalent in American society it is possible that at least some of the very poor may think that a change of customs is not worth the price of conformity or that nothing will come of it.

[23] See Hyman M. Fortstenzer, M.D., "Planning and Evaluation of Community Mental Health Problems," in U.S. Department of Health, Education, and Welfare, *Concepts of Community Psychiatry*, p. 140:

One approach which I favor, but which has not yet been accepted by all the planning groups, is based on acceptance of the value systems developed in the general public health field. Control of mental disorders is a public health problem, and our nation's largest health problem by any yardstick; the rate at which these disorders occur in the population; the number of people afflicted at any given moment of time; the economic cost to the individual, his family, his community, his government; the number of people incapacitated by their disorders to such a degree that they must be hospital-

try one is confronted with the widespread dearth of mental health services for all but the most privileged. The multiple task of developing remedial service for the individual child, for the parent, and for the family in need must, therefore, be attempted if this generation of human beings is to be given the services that in themselves may provide preventive health benefits for the next generation. One must also ask whether the concept of separating preventive from remedial mental health services does not involve an oversimplification. It has been wisely said that "very often what is cure for one is prevention for another."[24] Certainly in the field of law we have learned that only by providing justice to one individual do we develop the guidelines by which the perpetration and perpetuation of injustice to others can be prevented.

As one reads the new literature in both law and psychiatry which seeks to explore ways in which law and psychiatry may reach out to meet the needs of human beings, one is struck by a central value—the human worth of the individual. The importance of the feeling of worth and the necessity of modifying those conditions and institutions which diminish man's sense of his worth is the recurring theme.

As psychiatry and the social sciences move forward in the pursuit of knowledge and in their integrative efforts, understanding of law as an agent of social change rather than as the negating hand of the past should become a source of new strength. Indeed, the needs of the time have been reflected in laws that require greater knowledge and service to the community than either psychiatry or the social sciences are presently geared to provide.

While it is easier to write laws than to provide models or services, it must be recognized that both the new laws and the programs for the poor have been born of suffering, strife, and sacrifice far beyond those demanded of any professional group. They

ized; or the total effects of the disorders on society. Public health, while aiming for the ultimate ideal of optimum health for all people, concentrates on present needs, recognizing that limitation of effort to the programs of highest priority is a limitation of goals and should be temporary.

[24] Duhl, "The Psychiatric Revolution," p. 27.

did not spring full blown from the Minerva-like wisdom of any statesman or his bright young staff. They are the result of long struggles by men and women to secure their right and the right of their children to freedom and a sense of worth. For the most part, these people are anonymous: their names will not appear in history or even learned journals, yet their voices have been heard.

A new generation of professionals in law, the social sciences, and psychiatry faces the challenge of translating into action its commitment to the worth of the individual, long embodied (or embalmed) in our Constitution, now rediscovered and rewritten into law. Action too little and too late will prevent, postpone, or negate the promise of the law. Some experts in mental health find many referrals for new types of service perplexing and inappropriate. Understandably, they stress the need for appropriate requests for help if their expertise is to be used effectively. It sometimes seems that they are overly self-protective and need, above all else, to feel comfortable in the tasks assigned them. At the risk of being regarded as an unscientific outsider, I would say that the social disorders that we face show that more and more professionals must face discomfort with greater and greater fortitude. While professional integrity is to be respected, the refusal to enter uncharted, unsettling areas of undefined and unknown challenge does not fall into that category.

Community psychiatry means many things to many psychiatrists, as justice under law means many things to many lawyers, ranging from the extension of the practice of psychiatry to those who need it, to comprehensive mental health centers to provide a variety of preventive, therapeutic, and rehabilitative services for the individual, to participation in the planning and implementing of the new forms of social organization necessary to prevent mental illness and strengthen mental health. The process of organizational change, the development of manpower, the training of new personnel, and the creation of different values and attitudes cannot be quickly achieved.

As wisely put by Dr. Frank T. Rafferty, the eradication of human isolation and alienation is becoming a goal: "Development of the institutionalized means [of achieving this goal] remains in doubt, but it is an act of faith for many that human society will find a way to defend itself in some manner other than by attack, isolation, or alienation."[25] In the past, members of both the legal and psychiatric professions have too often served, and even supported, institutions that have denied justice and the full opportunity for mental health to the mentally ill, the deviant, and the poor. Today there is new hope that they will in ever growing numbers be moved to play a far different role in a world in which the value of human life will become of ever greater meaning.

[25] Frank T. Rafferty, M.D., "The Community Is Becoming," *American Journal of Orthopsychiatry*, XXXVI, No. 1 (January, 1966), 110.

Index

171

Designed by Arlene J. Sheer
Composed in Times Roman by Monotype Composition Company, Inc.
Printed offset by Universal Lithographers, Inc., on P & S R
Bound by the Maple Press Company in Columbia Riverside Linen